JOURNAL FOR THE STUDY OF THE OLD TESTAMENT SUPPLEMENT SERIES
281

Sheffield Academic Press

Isaiah 34–35

A Nightmare/A Dream

Peter D. Miscall

Journal for the Study of the Old Testament
Supplement Series 281

Published by Sheffield Academic Press Ltd
Mansion House
19 Kingfield Road
Sheffield S11 9AS
England

Printed on acid-free paper in Great Britain
by Bookcraft Ltd
Midsomer Norton, Bath

British Library Cataloguing in Publication Data

A catalogue record for this book is available
from the British Library

ISBN 1-85075-987-1

CONTENTS

ABBREVIATIONS

AnBib	Analecta biblica
ANET	James B. Pritchard (ed.), *Ancient Near Eastern Texts Relating to the Old Testament* (Princeton, NJ: Princeton University Press, 3rd edn, 1969)
BETL	Bibliotheca ephemeridum theologicarum lovaniensium
BHS	*Biblia hebraica stuttgartensia*
BO	*Bibliotheca orientalis*
BKAT	Biblischer Kommentar: Altes Testament
EncJud	*Encyclopedia Judaica* (12 vols.; Jerusalem: Keter Publishing, 1972)
GKC	*Gesenius' Hebrew Grammar* (ed. E. Kautzsch, revised and trans. A.E. Cowley; Oxford: Clarendon Press, 1910)
GNB	*Good News Bible*
JBL	*Journal of Biblical Literature*
JFA	*Journal of the Fantastic in the Arts*
JPS	Jewish Publication Society
JSOT	*Journal for the Study of the Old Testament*
JSOTSup	*Journal for the Study of the Old Testament*, Supplement Series
KJV	King James Version
NAB	*New American Bible*
NIV	New International Version
NJB	*New Jerusalem Bible*
NRSV	New Revised Standard Version
OTG	Old Testament Guides
OTL	Old Testament Library
REB	Revised English Bible
WBC	Word Biblical Commentary

Chapter 1

INTRODUCTION

A Way of Reading Isaiah

Discussions of Isaiah 34–35 usually concern their individual unity, authorship and date, and their relation to each other and to the rest of Isaiah, all on the assumption that they were written later than and separate from most of Isaiah 1–39. However, I propose to read them as a single poem that is an integral part of the entire book and vision of Isaiah that I regard as a whole work. Echoing others such as Vermeylen, Mathews refers to chs. 34–35 as a diptych, 'two poems in tandem…two halves of one whole' (1995: 12, 136-37). I concur and read 34–35 as one poem with contrasting scenes that I term the nightmare (34.1-15) and the dream (35.1-10). Even though my focus is on the chapters themselves, I will make comments on parallels with other parts of Isaiah to aid the analysis of Isaiah 34–35, to assess its place in Isaiah and to discuss some of the implications of this mode of reading for the study of the whole book of Isaiah. I employ a literary method that is a close reading combining grammatical and lexical information with poetic observations, such as parallelism and imagery, all placed in the larger framework of the flow and impact of the entire poem.[1]

For me, reading is a sequential and multiple process that struggles with content and form, that moves both through and back and forth in the poem with asides and digressions into other texts and matters. This results in a different, and I hope richer and more nuanced, appreciation and understanding of the poem. Thus I will be interspersing discussion of the poem itself and its text with wider ranging explications of the mode of reading, of the terms and concepts I employ and of the broader

---

1. I owe the approach to 34–35 as a two-part poem in part to a student, Chuck Zecher, particularly his treatment of 34.16-17 as a transition within the poem and not solely as a conclusion to ch. 34.

implications of this mode. I use the terms reading and interpretation more or less interchangeably to refer to this process. I am not trying to make a distinction such as between textual analysis (reading) and subsequent expansion or application (interpretation).

This is a departure from the usual treatments of the chapters that, as mentioned above, debate whether the two chapters are to be considered as one or two poems, whether each chapter is unified in itself regardless of its relation to the other, and when to date the composition of the poem or of its separate parts. For these various opinions, I refer my reader to Mathews's presentation (1995: 9-33, 155-79). I am not going to discuss them because I personally am about something fundamentally different than are the critics who propose them. I employ 'textual evidence', including repetitions, similarities, contrasts and shifts in terms, themes, images and parallels with and allusions to other texts to develop a reading of the poem—not to argue for or to prove the unity or disunity of the poem, nor to propose a date or series of dates for the composition of Isaiah 34–35. At points in this book I will discuss what other commentaries say to highlight, frequently by contrast, both my distinct way of reading and my specific interpretation of a word, phrase or passage.

As in my commentary and articles, I approach the book of Isaiah as a single work. I cite the following from my commentary as a partial explanation of my general approach.

> With Watts and Conrad I share the assumption of a unified work composed in the postexilic period, probably in the fifth century. However, I do not enter into further debate about date, authorship or the process of composition. I assume that the postexilic author(s) used much existing material, written and oral, some perhaps deriving from the eighth century, but I am not attempting to isolate any of that material, particularly original prophetic speeches. We have too little independent information about pre- or postexilic Israel to reconstruct a historical setting or process of writing except in the most general respects. I am offering an interpretation of Isaiah; I am not trying to prove a historical hypothesis (Miscall 1993: 11).

In this monograph I offer an interpretation of a poem—two chapters—in Isaiah with some attention given to the implications of this for reading all of Isaiah.

My approach assumes, on the part of 'Isaiah', a literary ability and sophistication to write a work—whether the poem in chs. 34–35 or the entire book of Isaiah—that includes (1) variation in all aspects, especially in style, terminology, theme, setting and imagery, and (2) a profound appreciation for a plural text that is rife with polysemy and ambiguity and that exists in an intertextual world. In this work, I use 'Isaiah' or 'the poet' as a shorthand for the composer(s) or author(s) of the book of Isaiah, whether Isaiah is thought of as an individual or a group. This is a way to avoid using terms such as 'author', 'editor' or 'redactor' that are laden with theoretical and historical judgments.

I turn now to describe briefly some of the major aspects of such an approach to Isaiah that are relevant to this study of Isaiah 34–35 (I will introduce others in the course of the analysis of the poem and will address the implications of the analysis for the book of Isaiah at points in the analysis and in my conclusion). The superscription to the book of Isaiah announces that the book is a vision, not a narrative work: 'The vision of Isaiah son of Amoz which he envisioned concerning Judah and Jerusalem'. Readers see and imagine what the book says just as much as they hear and understand it. Imagery—for example, imagery of water and fire and of crops and flocks—is an integral part of reading the book and will be central to our interpretation of Isaiah 34–35. I deal with imagery at greater length in the discussion of the poem, particularly in the treatment of 34.4 (see below, pp. 41-43). The vision of Isaiah is an imposing work of poetry that depicts and portrays God, the universe, all humanity and the gamut of history from creation onwards. Within this grand sweep the poet focuses on the fortunes of one people, Israel, in two critical periods of their history: first, the Assyrian invasions of the late eighth century BCE that result in the destruction of the northern kingdom and second, the Babylonian invasions of the late seventh and early sixth centuries BCE that result in the exile and are followed by the subsequent return from exile in Babylon in the latter half of the sixth century BCE.[2]

These periods, with their events and the peoples involved in them, become grand patterns and characters in the vision that takes on a strong dramatic aspect with its many speakers and speeches. 'Isaiah' composed this poetic vision known as the book of Isaiah sometime after these events and employs them to present the vision of God and humanity, of God's dealings with the world (especially the choice of

---

2. In this book, I use 'Israel' in the general sense of 'the people of God' without distinguishing between Israel, the northern kingdom, and Judah, the southern kingdom. The distinction is relevant to other parts of Isaiah, particularly in parts of chs. 1–39, but is not relevant to this reading of the poem in 34–35.

one people), and of what life lived on God's holy mountain might be like. This assumes a postexilic date for the composition of the book, but, as already noted, I am not thereby arguing for a particular date and setting for that composition or for a particular author, whether an individual or a group, or mode of composition.

Our historical knowledge is employed in this mode of reading, but not as a template that tells us what the text has to mean. I say 'our historical knowledge' and not 'history' because it is our knowledge, what we know and mainly what we know from other texts, that is brought to bear on reading Isaiah and not history perceived as objective facts that are either outside our knowing or totally separate from other texts and narratives. Hayden White's comments on the frequent attempt to distinguish the 'real' (history) from the 'imagined' (literature) are germane.

> Nor is it unusual for literary theorists, when they are speaking about the 'context' of a literary work, to suppose that this context—the 'historical mileu'—has a concreteness and an accessibility that the work itself can never have, as if it were easier to perceive the reality of a past world put together from a thousand historical documents than it is to probe the depths of a single literary work that is present to the critic studying it. But the presumed concreteness and accessibility of historical milieux, these contexts of the texts that literary scholars study, are themselves products of the fictive capability of the historians who have studied these contexts. The historical documents are not less opaque than the texts studied by the literary critic. Nor is the world those documents figure more accessible. The one is no more 'given' than the other. In fact, the opaqueness of the world figured in historical documents is, if anything, increased by the production of historical narratives. Each new historical work only adds to the number of possible texts that have to be interpreted if a full and accurate picture of a given historical milieu is to be faithfully drawn (1978: 89).

To illustrate the final sentence, I need only point to the large number of works that attempt to date the book of Isaiah both in its final form and in the stages of its development, and to the ongoing and heated controversy surrounding the very attempt to write a history of either pre-exilic or postexilic Israel or Palestine. Even a literary reading, such as the present one, is added to the stew that should produce 'a full and accurate picture' of ancient Israel.

For example, much of Isaiah 1–39 reflects the period of Israel's history extending from approximately 735 to 700 BCE as that period is narrated in other texts, whether those of 2 Kings or those of Noth,

Bright and Miller-Hayes. The period begins with the Syro-Ephraimite War of c. 735–732 that ends with Tiglath-pileser's destruction of Damascus and invasion of Israel, the northern kingdom. Israel was spared total conquest because Hoshea (732–722) paid tribute. Judah, ruled by Ahaz, apparently became a loyal Assyrian subject. Within a few years Israel rebelled against Assyria, was destroyed by the Assyrian king Sargon in 722 (see Isa. 20) and incorporated into the Assyrian empire. Judah remained a loyal subject state. Hezekiah succeeded Ahaz on the Judean throne in 715. In about 704 he joined another coalition against Assyria. Sennacherib, the Assyrian king of the time, invaded Judah in 701, devastated most of the country, besieged Jerusalem, but did not capture the city (Isa. 36–37).[3]

Isaiah, however, is not interested in relating a historical narrative but in displaying a vision. Therefore, the poet takes the events of 735–700 and compresses them into one of his major poetic images and patterns. Because of human evil, YHWH plans an invasion of the world and of Israel and Judah with resultant widespread devastation that still leaves a surviving remnant (Isa. 1.7-9). An overwhelming force sweeps through the land (5.26-30) and, taking on the form of the Assyrian army, destroys all before it including Damascus and Israel. It rushes into Judah like a swarm of insects (7.18-19). The force is like a flood that reaches to the neck (8.8), but leaves the head as the image of the survivors and as an image of Jerusalem (chs. 36–37).

> And daughter Zion is left like a booth in a vineyard,
> Like a lodge in a cucumber field, like a besieged city (1.8).[4]

This poetic pattern of invasion and survivors also appears in the image of the forest being cut down and the remaining stumps producing new shoots (10.15–11.1). Once the Assyrian is removed, the overwhelming force takes on the form of the king and city of Babylon (13.17–14.23; 39). Babylon destroys Judah and Jerusalem and takes all away; 'nothing is left' (39.6). Finally the unstoppable army transmutes into the positive form of Cyrus who sweeps away the Babylonians and allows the restoration of the people and the rebuilding of the city.

The overall pattern and its stages can be recast into the contrast of

3.   I recognize that even this brief summary of 735–700 BCE could be questioned according to the issues raised by White (1978), but I leave these questions of history for another work.

4.   See p. 45 n. 17.

times and scenes of invasion and resultant devastation with those of
restoration and return. The book of Isaiah is notable for its alternation
and juxtaposition of such scenes, and such juxtaposition is directly relevant to our poem and its contrast of nightmare and dream. This larger
pattern is further enriched and complicated since it overlaps, at many
points, with the distinction between righteousness and sin that should
respectively result in prosperity and destruction. The vision of Isaiah
opens with denunciation of Israel's rebellion, followed by descriptions
of the beaten people using metaphors of the human body, and of the
desolate land that is easy pickings for the enemy.

> Hear, O heavens! and give ear, O earth! for YHWH speaks:
> Children I rear and bring up, but they rebel against me.
> The ox knows its owner, and the donkey the crib of its master;
> Israel does not know, my people do not understand.
> Woe! Sinful nation; iniquitous people;
> offspring of evil-doers; children who act corruptly!
> They have forsaken YHWH; they have despised the Holy One of Israel;
>   they have turned back.
> On what can you be beaten further that you continue to rebel?
> The whole head is sick and the whole heart faint...
> Your country is a desolation; your cities are burning in fire; your land: in
>   your very presence aliens eat it (1.2-7).

Near the close of the first chapter, the poet denounces Jerusalem who
is figured as a woman in this passage and throughout the vision of
Isaiah. She and her leaders are guilty of violence and exploitation of the
helpless. YHWH punishes them with a smelting process that, by implication, removes the wicked and leaves the faithful; the implication is
confirmed in the closing statement. The smelting process concludes
with restoration.

> How she has become a whore! The Capital Faithful!
> She was full of justice, righteousness lodged in her—but now
>   murderers...
> Your princes are rebels and companions of thieves...
> They do not deal justly with the orphan and they do not hear the
>   widow's plea.
> Therefore says the lord, YHWH of Hosts, the Bull of Israel:
> Woe! I am comforted concerning my enemies and I am avenged
>   concerning my foes!
> I turn my hand against you, I smelt away your dross as though using lye
>   and I remove all your alloy.

I return your judges as at the beginning and your counselors as at the
  first.
Then you will be called The City of Righteousness, The Capital Faithful.
Zion is redeemed by justice and those who return to her, by
  righteousness,
But rebels and sinners are destroyed together and those who forsake
  YHWH are consumed (1.21-28).

This principle of retributive justice is important for the reading of the
poem, notably 34.1-9, and the question of possible motivations for
YHWH's wrath. Are the nations simply destroyed or is this punishment
for sin?

The passage at the close of ch. 1 is followed, almost immediately, by
the vision of the latter days when all humanity comes to the mountain
of YHWH's house. Even though this is a vision of a future time, it is a
vision that we see now and therefore I translate using the present tense.

This will be in the latter times:
The mountain of the house of YHWH is established
As tallest of the mountains, as the highest of the hills,
And all the nations flow to it, many peoples come and say,
'Come, let us go up to the mountain of YHWH, to the house of the God
  of Jacob
That he may teach us his ways and that we may walk in his paths
For teaching comes forth from Zion and the word of YHWH from
  Jerusalem'.[5]
He judges among the nations and decides for many peoples;
They beat their swords into plowshares and their spears into pruning
  hooks;
Nation does not lift a sword against nation, and they no longer learn war
  (2.2-4).

This inclusion of all humanity, Israel and the nations, in Isaiah's
vision of God and the world is another significant theme since Isaiah
alternates descriptions of the status and fate of Israel and the nations
and then at points combines the two into humanity or 'all flesh' (see
40.5; 66.23-24). This vision of 'all the nations' is immediately followed
by denunciations of 'the house of Jacob' (2.5-8) and of all human pride
and arrogance without any distinction of nations (2.9-22). 'The haughty
eyes of humanity are brought low; proud people are humbled—YHWH
alone is exalted on that day' (2.11).

---

5.   KJV and GNB include the last part of v. 3 in the peoples' exhortation as in
my translation; most other translations close the quotation after 'in his paths'.

This inclusiveness is an important feature in reading Isaiah. YHWH is against all human pride and arrogance, not just that of the nations. On the other hand, YHWH acts for the benefit of all poor and needy, not just Israel. The following passages can refer to Israel or Israelites but they are not restricted to reference to Israel alone.

> The poor and the needy are seeking water and there is none; their tongue
> is parched with thirst.
> I YHWH answer them; I the God of Israel do not forsake them (41.17).

> I lead the blind on a road they don't know; on paths they don't know I
> guide them.
> The darkness before them I turn to light; the rough places into level
> ground—these things I do; I don't abandon them (42.16).

> This is the one I look upon: the poor and broken in spirit, the one who
> trembles at my word (66.2).

This is a form of the relation of the general and the particular. What holds for all humanity holds for Israel, the nations or appropriate human groups and, vice versa, what holds for any one of the latter, including Israel, can hold for all humanity. This will be relevant to our reading of Isaiah 34–35 when we face the question of who and what are the object of the devastation described in 34.1-15 and of the restoration in 35.1-10. I do not read Isaiah as a clear and simplistic morality tale in which Israel is ultimately saved and restored and all the other nations are destroyed or subjected to Israel, even though such a morality tale is a part of the vision of Isaiah. That is, there are passages that assert it, but they are then contrasted with or contradicted by passages that portray prosperity and restoration for all or at least for all who are righteous, who are YHWH's servants. There are also the grim passages, such as 2.11, in which YHWH comes in wrath against the world and all humanity.

> Look! YHWH is stripping the earth bare and emptying it; he twists its
> surface and scatters its inhabitants...
> The earth is stripped bare and it is totally plundered
> For YHWH speaks this word.
> The earth dries up, it withers; the world shrivels, it withers; the heavens
> shrivel with the earth (24.1-4).

> Look! YHWH comes in fire, and like a whirlwind, his chariots,
> To return his anger as fury and his rebuke as flames of fire.
> Yes, by fire—by his sword—YHWH enters into judgment with all flesh;
> and many are those slain by YHWH (66.15-16).

On the other hand, Isaiah is not a clear tale of retributive justice in which all the righteous and good, regardless of what nation they belong to, are rewarded and prosper and only the wicked and evil are punished and perish. This is, as is the tale of saved Israel and doomed nations, both asserted and then contradicted. Indeed, it is contradicted by passages that assert Israel's favored status; YHWH's choice of Israel has nothing to do with the latter's goodness or worthiness.

> You, Israel, my servant; Jacob, whom I have chosen; children of
> Abraham whom I love;
> Whom I brought with strength from the ends of the earth and called from
> its farthest reaches.
> And I said to you, 'You are my servant; I chose you and did not reject
> you' (41.8-9).

I will discuss further this topic of Israel and the nations and destruction and restoration in the course of the reading of our poem.

Why Isaiah 34–35?

As Mathews notes (1995: 6-8), scholars have long focused on these two chapters because they appear distinct from their context and because they share terminology and explicit contrasts, especially that between the devastation of 34 and the joy and transformation of 35. Duhm and others referred to them as the 'Little Apocalypse' and compared them with Isaiah 24–27, the so-called 'Isaiah Apocalypse'.[6] Regardless of the positions taken on the unity of the two chapters, their authorship and date(s) of composition, there is a strong tendency in contemporary scholarship to focus on the two chapters as an example of a general prophetic pattern of judgment on the nations and salvation for Israel. 'It is easy to read the chapters as two sides of the same coin: Yahweh's judgment on the nations means prosperity for Israel' (Barton 1995: 93). Within this general prophetic pattern, there is a wide variety of opinion on the precise relationship of the chapters or of each of them separately to other parts of Isaiah; this is especially so with ch. 35, which has close ties of vocabulary, theme and imagery with 40–66. 35.10 is repeated in 51.11.

This critical focus initially drew my attention to these two chapters. Over time the attention to the two chapters was augmented by the real-

6. See Barton 1995: 92-95 for an overview of the study of the chapters including a defense of the title 'Little Apocalypse'.

ization that they stand in the physical center of the book and can perhaps tell us something about the whole book. Other factors that kept my attention were the vivid imagery of both waste and restoration and the changing styles of the poem. Following are other specific points that explain why I concern myself with 34–35 as a poem. First, ch. 34 opens with a call to nations and peoples to pay attention; this marks a break with the close of ch. 33. Second, ch. 34 opens with the demand for movement, 'Draw near!', and 35 closes with a description of movement as the ransomed return; the poem is thereby enclosed by the motif of movement. Third, ch. 36 opens with a notice of a date and an attack. The shift in style, like that in 34.1, marks the beginning of a new section.

Finally, my continued work with the poem both in itself and in its context in Isaiah has convinced me that pursuing a close reading of it is a worthwhile project both for the poem itself and for the implications for reading the entire book of Isaiah. However, this does not mean that I am arguing for the poem as a separate or independent work. Isaiah 34–35 is an integral part of the whole book and of the immediate context, and my focus on the one poem is, in many ways, due to heuristic and practical concerns. The study is productive of many insights, particular and general, because the poem is large and rich enough and yet not too large. I could do a similar close reading of other segments such as chs. 33–35 and 32–37 but that would expand this work beyond manageable limits. Unlike most other studies of Isaiah, I am not attempting to establish only one way of outlining, dividing or structuring the book.

Text, Translation and Poetry

The initial basis of the study is the Hebrew text of *BHS*, including its arrangement of the poem into lines that are subdivided into cola by spaces. In the course of the reading, I note and discuss in varying detail many departures from the Hebrew text and this poetic arrangement, whether or not I incorporate them into my translation and analysis.[7] (As a general principle, I approach text-critical issues, mainly different readings witnessed in other Hebrew manuscripts and in the versions, as much more a matter of treating alternative understandings and interpretations of a text than a process of establishing a correct or original text.)

---

7.   Unless the vocalization of a word is necessary for the presentation, I print only the consonantal text of Hebrew terms and phrases.

This procedure has the advantage of starting with a known and available text, but I do recognize that *BHS* represents editorial decisions (interpretations) about how to print the Hebrew text of Isaiah from a tenth-century CE manuscript that does not exhibit such poetic form and that is itself a product of centuries of copying, recopying and annotating. Indeed, it is only in twentieth-century Bibles that poetic sections, such as psalms and prophetic literature, are printed consistently in poetic form.[8]

My translations are literal, but I do not render the exact Hebrew, in particular the word order, if it would result in a wooden or grammatically incorrect English translation. However, I do occasionally include in brackets words that are implied by the Hebrew but not actually in it; I explain the addition in a note. At many points in the analysis I offer alternative translations of a colon or longer section. The translation of the entire poem presented after this introduction is akin to the Hebrew text printed in *BHS* in the sense that both are starting-points for ongoing analysis and interpretation, but are not end products that present the one true translation or interpretation of the poem. This is the main reason why I do not close my monograph by printing this or a revised translation: being placed at the end would give it too much the appearance of a set conclusion, the best and perhaps only way to translate the poem.

The translation includes not just the English words and phrases used to render the Hebrew, but also the entire presentation on the page: poetic or prose form; all the punctuation marks; use of capital letters; spacing within and between lines and sections of lines; the use of other dividing marks, as found in English Bibles, such as chapter and verse; and other headings for chapters and other divisions. Even though the present system of chapters and verses was added to the biblical text in the late Middle Ages to facilitate reference and cross-reference, it can still influence or even determine aspects of our reading of a book of the Bible. For example, a large bold-faced **35** following a noticeable space after Isa. 34.17 leads a reader to assume that what follows is somehow different from the preceding. To offset this effect I print the full translation of the poem without chapter or verse numbering and, further, I

---

8. For example, in Isaiah, GNB prints most of chs. 1–39 in prose form and most of 40–66 in poetic form. Chapter 34 is presented as prose and 35 as poetry. Such a shift in form almost requires readers of the GNB to treat the two chapters as separate sections.

do not give a title to the full poem since this would lead to a focus on the elements of the title.[9] However, in the analysis itself I indicate verses and subdivisions marked with a, b, c, and so on, to make it clear the exact part of the poem that I am referring to.

The separate sections of the poem that I print and then comment on represent significant portions of material but not a claim that this is the only way to divide and subdivide the poem, that this is *the structure* of the poem. This is analogous to my focus on Isaiah 34–35 as a significant section in the book of Isaiah. I acknowledge my indebtedness to Roland Barthes's *S/Z* for this particular insight and for the initial understanding and practice of reading that inform this analysis of Isaiah 34–35.[10]

My understanding of Hebrew poetry, especially parallelism and rhythm, shares much with Petersen's and Richards's presentation. The basic unit is the line or colon, not the bicolon or tricolon (Petersen and Richards 1992: 23). 'Approach, O Nations, to hear!' is a line or colon while

> Approach, O Nations, to hear!
> O Peoples, pay attention!

is a bicolon. I see larger units, for example, a tetracolon or quatrain such as 34.10, in this poem and regard them not as essential elements or structures of Hebrew poetry, but as examples of poetic diversity. In my format, I indicate the opening colon of a poetic set by setting it flush left; the next colon or cola are indented. Within a verse of the MT, each colon represents a section noted as a, b, c, and so on, in the analysis, even though my poetic divisions don't always match the verse divisions of the MT.

The balance between cola can be measured in terms both of stressed words and of syllables; I only touch on this in my analysis.[11] However,

9.   Watts (1987: 2-5) prints 34–35 as one text with no space between the chapters and with minimal intrusion of verse numbers. However, he makes the distinction in his bold-faced, large-type heading: 'Edom's Curse–Judah's Renewal'.

10.   Barthes refers to this as cutting up the text 'into a series of brief, contiguous fragments, which we shall call *lexias*, since they are units of reading' (1974: 13).

11.   I look for balance and not equivalence in syllables and accented words. The establishment of any firm system of determining 'line length' is limited by the gaps in our knowledge of the vocalization of ancient Hebrew and of whether there were any features or poetic conventions, such as elision or linking, employed in reading poetry.

my grasp of the rhythm and scansion is reflected in my translation in the division of the poem into cola and in the placement of the cola into larger groupings. I employ poetic, semantic and grammatical features in deciding on cola and their interrelationships. I comment at points on other possible scansions if they affect the reading. I reiterate an earlier point that such scansion and poetic, grammatical analysis are all parts of the interpretation that I am presenting; they are not an objective, value-free process that subjective reading is then applied to. In addition, I emphasize the balance and tension between variety and regularity (Petersen and Richards 1992: 70-71) present in this poem in all aspects: grammatical, semantic (especially words) and poetic. Indeed, repeated words or phrases stand out against the background of a consistently different vocabulary.

I note other poetic features, such as assonance, chiasmus and punning, at points for their own sake or to buttress a reading, but I am not presenting a thorough treatment of the poem at this level. Muilenberg's literary study of Isaiah 34, often noted but seldom engaged, is solid in this area and I could only repeat and nuance his analysis and examples;[12] indeed, many of my examples are his or expansions of his.

A solid understanding and appreciation of Hebrew poetry has to take all of these aspects—parallelism, rhythm, line structure, assonance, word play, figurative language—into account at once, and cannot privilege just one or two features—usually parallelism and line structure—as the definition of Hebrew poetry. The prevalence of figurative language is just as much a characteristic difference between biblical poetry and prose as parallelism. Genesis opens by speaking about the heavens and the earth as physical realms created by God, whereas Isaiah opens by addressing them as personifications that have ears to hear. Biblical poetry, not just Isaiah, is marked by the consistent use of a wide variety of such tropes, for example, personification or prosopopoeia and its frequently accompanying apostrophe, simile, metaphor and synecdoche.

The comments and discussion that follow the printed portion of the poem are usually divided into two sections with some necessary overlap. First is a verse-by-verse analysis of specific issues of grammar,

---

12. Particularly useful are his lists of specific literary features such as paronomasia, word sets, parallelism of words and phrases, etc. (Muilenberg 1940: 357-64 [1984: 77-84]).

syntax, text, translation, poetic form, scansion, and so on. This is followed by discussion of larger scale issues of content and form, placement in Isaiah, allusions to other parts of the Hebrew Bible and of the
assumptions and implications of this mode of reading. This division
begins to break down as we progress in our reading of the poem.

A Fantastic Way of Reading Isaiah

Thanks to the pioneering efforts of scholars such as George Aichele
and Tina Pippin, categories and terminology drawn from the contemporary study of fantasy are now being applied to the interpretation of the
Bible.[13] Fantasy as a literary genre is broad and includes both the positive works that are like fairy-tales and that are usually referred to as
'fantasy' and the negative works of horror and terror. I draw from and
expand upon my two articles 'Biblical Narrative and Categories of the
Fantastic' (Miscall 1992a) and 'Isaiah: Dreams and Nightmares, Fantasy and Horror' (Miscall 1997) to clarify how the study of the fantastic
contributes to this reading of Isaiah 34–35.

The fantastic as a term and literary category is derived from
Todorov's seminal study in which he situates the fantastic between two
other genres. In the *uncanny*, 'the laws of reality remain intact and
permit an explanation of the phenomena described', while in the
marvelous, 'new laws of nature must be entertained to account for the
phenomena' (Todorov 1973: 41). The latter can include supernatural
explanations. In the fantastic, character(s) and reader(s) experience an
unresolved hesitation between these two explanations: reality or dream,
natural event or supernatural miracle. This profound hesitation is
expanded in many of the readings of the Bible to include much post-
modern critical wrestling with alternative and often contradictory
readings of a given text. I will detail my particular use of hesitation at
relevant points in the reading of Isaiah 34–35.

Aichele maintains that

> For the modernist *episteme*… fantasy lies at or perhaps beyond the limits
> of the possible. It is non-realistic. Literary fantasy presents, as though it
> were real, an alternative reality—an escape from reality (1997: 178; his
> emphasis).

---

13. For further discussion and bibliography, see the two journal issues that they
have co-edited: *Semeia* 60 (1992) and *JFA* 8 (1997).

The escape can be constructive or destructive depending on whether the fantasy leads to liberation or flight from the responsibilities of life. However, for an alternative to this modernist view, Aichele turns to Todorov's theory of the fantastic as hesitation or oscillation between radically different interpretations of a text. Todorov presents

> a postmodern theory which redefines the relation between fantasy and reality. In fantasy, narrative becomes 'aware' of itself as fiction, and it speaks its own inescapable fictionality... It resists coherent reading and makes the reader aware of how much she contributes to the telling of the tale... It reveals the violence done to the text by interpretation (Aichele 1997: 178-79).

Through this theory our attention is drawn to the text itself that projects this fantasy world and leaves us caught between competing readings. The materiality of the text includes the words that compose the text and even the letters of the alphabet that compose the words. Perhaps close enough attention to them in their sequence can help resolve the problem and move us beyond the hesitation. We will read Isaiah 34–35 with such attention and find that it still leaves us with our reading options open. And there will be other ways, including word-play and text-critical issues, in which the material text will be central to the reading and I will comment on them as we progress.

For me, however, much of the contribution of the study of the fantastic lies in the area of the different terms employed and the changed perspective on biblical material that they permit. As I note in my article on Isaiah,

> Reading Isaiah through lenses of the Fantastic, particularly those of fantasy and horror which I also term dream and nightmare, is a deliberate turn from the religious and theological dichotomies of righteousness and sin and the salvation and judgment to which they lead (1997: 151).

Simply to call Isaiah 34–35 a nightmare and a dream, or a horror tale and a fantasy, presents a new perspective on and set of expectations for a reading of the poem in place of those implied by the more common 'judgment on the nations and Edom' and 'salvation of Judah'. The full impact of this shift in critical vocabulary will be obvious as I progress through the poem.

My final point deals with my expansive style of reading that derives, in part, from reflection on Aichele's work. I extend his comments from narrative fantasy to include critical discourse such as this present analysis of Isaiah 34–35. Critical discourse in this mode 'makes the reader aware of how much she contributes to the telling of the tale...It reveals the violence done to the text by interpretation' (Aichele and Pippin 1997: 179). The expansive style reveals itself in the presentation of alternative readings, translations and presentations of the text and, in particular, in the citation of parallel texts.

Throughout this reading of the poem, I am open to ambiguity, polysemy and different levels of meaning; I reiterate that I am not trying to propose just one, focused way of reading the poem, or just one, specific interpretation of the poem. I want to explore and develop a large number of avenues that can lead both into the interpretation of the poem and out into considerations of reading Isaiah as a whole and of reading and interpretation themselves. However, for practical considerations of space, I pursue in detail a limited number of alternative interpretations and only point to others as possible; I leave it to my readers to pursue them if they wish.

For example, I cite a significant number of passages from Isaiah and a much smaller number from other parts of the Hebrew Bible; the parallels serve a variety of purposes such as demonstrating the range of usage of a form, for example, the initial call, the range of usage and meaning of terms or whether or not a specific phrase or image is characteristic of Isaiah. But the passages cited, in themselves and in their own contexts, contain much more of direct and indirect relevance to Isaiah 34–35 than what I discuss in citing them, and I leave this extra information, this supplement, in my own text as a strong reminder that the focus and limits of this study are part of what I contribute to the retelling of the poem, part of the violence that I, the interpreter, do to this text. Whether a reading is tight and centered or loose and expansive (such as mine) is, in large part, the interpreter's choice and is not something forced or required by the text analyzed.[14]

14. I leave open the theoretical and practical issues marked by the phrase 'in large part'. I am not advocating a style of interpretation in which the interpreter has total and absolute control. In my article 'Texts, More Texts, a Textual Reader and a Textual Writer', I reflect on the intertextual and plural nature of both reading and writing (Miscall 1995).

The Poem

Approach, O Nations, to hear!
O Peoples, pay attention!
Let the earth and all that fills it hear,
the world and all that springs from it.
Yes, wrath for YHWH against all the nations
and fury against all their armies.
He has doomed them,
he has given them to the slaughter.
Their slain are thrown out
and their corpses: their stench goes up.
The mountains melt with their blood
and all the armies of the heavens rot;
The heavens roll up like a scroll,
and all their armies wither
Like leaves wither from the vine,
like [a leaf] withering from the fig tree.
Yes, my sword drank its fill in the heavens!
Now it comes down on Edom,
yes, on my doomed people, for judgment.
A sword for YHWH:
it is filled with blood,
it is gorged with fat,
With the blood of lambs and goats,
with the fat of the innards of rams.
Yes, a sacrifice for YHWH in Bozrah,
and a great slaughter in the land of Edom.
Wild oxen go down with them,
and young bulls with bulls;
Their land drinks its fill of blood,
and their dust is gorged with fat.
Yes, a day of vengeance for YHWH,
a year of retribution for Zion's case.
Her wadis turn to pitch,
and her dust to brimstone.
And her land is
burning pitch.
Night and day it does not extinguish;
forever her smoke goes up;
from generation to generation she is desolate;
for an eternity of eternities none pass through her.
But they possess her, the desert owl and the screech owl,
and the great owl and the raven dwell in her;

He stretches over her the line of desolation,
>   and the weights of nothingness [next to] her nobles;
There is Not There a Kingdom they name [her],
>   and all her princes are Nothing.
For thorns go up over her fortresses;
>   nettles and brambles in her strongholds.
And she is a pasture for jackals,
>   grass for ostriches.
Demons meet with phantoms,
>   and a hairy beast calls to [meet with] his friend.
Indeed there Lilith reposes
>   and finds for herself rest.
There the owl nests and delivers
>   for she hatches and broods in her shade.
Indeed there vultures gather,
>   each with her friend.
Seek from the scroll of YHWH and read:
>   Not one of these is missing!
[Each with her friend, they do not decide
>   because 'my mouth', it has commanded]
>   and his breath, it has gathered them.
And it has cast for them the lot,
>   and his hand has divided her for them with the line.
Forever they will possess her,
>   for generation to generation they will dwell in her.
Let wilderness and dry land rejoice;
>   desert, shout and bloom;
Like the crocus, let her bloom luxuriantly;
>   let her shout, shout aloud, yea, sing!
The glory of the Lebanon is given to her,
>   the splendor of the Carmel and the Sharon.
They see the glory of YHWH,
>   the splendor of our God.
Strengthen weak hands
>   and faltering knees firm up;
Say to trembling hearts:
>   Be strong! Do not fear!
See! Your God!
>   Vengeance comes!
Divine retaliation!
>   It comes and saves you!
Then are opened the eyes of the blind
>   and the ears of the deaf are opened.
Then the lame leap like deer
>   and the tongue of the speechless sings.

Indeed waters break forth in the wilderness
    and streams in the desert.
And the burning sand is a swamp,
    and the thirsty ground, springs of water.
In the pasture of jackals is her resting place;
    [her] grass [turns] to reed and rush.
There emerges there a highway, yes, a way;
    The Holy Way it is called to her.
The unclean do not pass over it;
    it is for him/them who walk(s) the way;
    fools do not wander [on it].
There is not there a lion,
    nor does a ravenous beast go up on it;
    she is not found there.
But they walk, the redeemed,
    yes, the ransomed of YHWH, they return;
They come to Zion with song,
    yes, everlasting joy on their heads.
Rejoicing and joy, they attain
    and they flee, grief and sighing.

Chapter 2

READING THE POEM

The Nightmare

34.1-3b

1   Approach, O Nations, to hear!
        O[1] Peoples, pay attention!
    Let the earth and all that fills it hear,
        the world and all that springs from it.
2   Yes, wrath for YHWH against all the nations
        and fury against all their armies.
    He has doomed them,
        he has given them to the slaughter.
3   Their slain are thrown out
        and their corpses: their stench goes up.

I treat the first four lines as a pair of closely connected bicola—perhaps even a tetracolon or quatrain—because of the content. The structure of this quatrain demonstrates the poet's use of variety. The first bicolon is enclosed by the imperatives—the structure is $a{:}b{:}c{:}{:}b_1{:}a_1$—that are joined by assonance: קִרְבוּ; and הַקְשִׁיבוּ; the second bicolon has one verb and repeats the subjects: $a{:}b{:}c{:}{:}b_1{:}c_1$.

All humanity and the whole earth are summoned to listen to the poet. The opening grammatical construction, an imperative with an infinitive construct, occurs in a call in 42.18: 'O you blind, look to see'. This is just one of the poet's variations on the call to pay attention as it occurs in the book of Isaiah (see below, pp. 33-35). The two waws in the last two cola of v. 1 can be understood as explicative or epexegetical (Waltke and O'Connor 1990: 648-49, 652-53) emphasizing that not only the entire earth hears but all that is in it. 'Let the earth, and yes, all that fills it hear, the world, and yes, all that springs from it'. תשׁמע is

---

1.   Following translations such as JPS, NAB and NRSV, I render the *waw* as part of the vocative: O! NIV, NJB and REB translate analogously with 'you peoples'.

usually taken as a jussive, 'let hear', but the two cola in 1d-e can also
be taken as a consequent or attendant effect on nature of the human
listening. In this sense it is translated 'the earth hears' or 'will hear'
with the latter more in the sense of an ongoing state than of a simple
future: 'The earth will hear and all that fills it'.

There is no grammatical marker of the jussive in the Hebrew word
and therefore this one term can carry these various English translations.
Coupled with the alternative ways of translating the two waws, this
produces a variety of ways of understanding and translating just this
one bicolon. Since polysemy, from individual words to the whole
poem, is a hallmark of my reading, I do not argue for one translation as
preferable or better than another. However, I do have to print one and
not the others in my opening translation of the poem and I recognize
that this will give that particular rendering preference in this study and
for its readers.

Verse 1 is inclusive: humanity (nations and peoples) and the world
are called together; world is referred to by the pair ארץ and תבל (see
18.3 and 24.4 for the same pair). The nouns 'that fills' and 'that springs
from' are not a bound pair elsewhere in Isaiah, but they do occur in
close proximity in ch. 42 in reverse order and in a similar, all-inclusive
context.

> Thus says the God, YHWH, who creates the heavens, who stretches them
> out, who spreads the earth and *what springs from it* (v. 5; see 44.3).

> Sing to YHWH a new song…those who go down to the sea and those
> *who fill it*; the coastlands and those who dwell in them (v. 10).

The heavens are not summoned in 34.1 as in the call to both heavens
and earth in 1.2. However, the heavens will soon be on the scene in
34.4.

The call is in the present and we, the readers, are included, at least to
the extent that we listen and read and then watch or imagine the
scene(s), the vision, that the poet displays before us. In a sense we read
and watch looking over the shoulders of the nations. The vision is present, is now, even when it refers to the future. The grim land of ch. 34
exists forever and the redeemed return in the future but we, the readers,
see both happening now. In my translation I attempt to capture this
visionary aspect, this presentness, by avoiding the consistent use of the
future tense employed in most translations. (My translations of the passages from chs. 1–2 on pp. 14-15 employ this practice.) As I progress

through the poem, this will give a different hue to the scenes described.

'Yes' attempts to capture the force of כִּי as both an emphatic adverb and a conjunction (Waltke and O'Connor 1990: 657, 665)—that is, the two bicola following the particle both explain the preceding call, 'for' or 'because', and emphasize the divine violence, 'indeed'. Even though one meaning, an adverb or a conjunction, may be clearly dominant in any given context, the other(s) are still latent in the Hebrew term. This is similar to my preceding discussion of תִּשְׁמַע where jussive and future senses inhere in the one word; it is in the English translation that we usually have to choose only one meaning.

Wrath (קֶצֶף) and fury (חֵמָה) are both often used in the latter portion of Isaiah.[2] 'Wrath for YHWH' is the first of four phrases that ascribe something to YHWH using a *lamedh* and not a construct (see 'the scroll of YHWH' in 34.16 for the latter syntax): wrath; a sword (v. 6a); a sacrifice (6e); and a day of vengeance (8). The first and the last two phrases are introduced forcefully by כִּי. Watts (1987: 5, 8-9) claims that this grammatical form, rather than the construct, emphasizes possession which connotes the royal prerogative of the divine monarch (see 33.22). He renders all four occurrences similar to the first: 'Surely Yahweh (has a right) to wrath on all nations'. My translation stresses YHWH's possession but not his royal or divine right since I see no reflection of this elsewhere in the poem. I render all four phrases similarly to reveal the repetition in the Hebrew.

In reference to v. 6, 'a sword for YHWH', Wildberger comments that 'this should not be translated "the sword of Yahweh", as too often happens, for the latter is the familiar חֶרֶב יְהוָה' (1982: 1327). He renders the four phrases differently in their contexts not choosing to reveal the literal repetition: 'Jahwe hat einer Zorn über all Völker' ('Yhwh has wrath for all nations'), 'Ein Schwert führt Jahwe' ('Yhwh brings a sword'), 'Denn ein Opferfest hält Jahwe' ('For Yhwh holds a sacrifice') and 'Denn Jahwe hat einer Tag der Rache' (For Yhwh has a day of vengeance'). Other English translations render the four phrases, with

---

2.   Wrath: 47.6; 54.8-9; 57.16-17; 60.10. Fury: 27.4; 42.25; 51.13, 17, 20, 22; 59.18; 63.3-6; 66.15. Anger (עֶבְרָה) is not present in our poem despite the play with the consonants ב, ר and ע in vv. 9-11 and 35.1; עֶבְרָה occurs in 9.18; 10.6; 13.9, 13; 14.6 and 16.6. Isa. 9.17-18 describes a massive fire that is similar to the scene in 34.9-10: 'Wickedness indeed burns like fire; it consumes briers and thorns; It kindles the thickets of the forest; they billow up in a column of smoke. Through the *anger* of YHWH of hosts the land was scorched and the people became like fuel for the fire.'

the possible exception of the first, similarly as I and Watts do (see NAB, NRSV and REB) or varied as Wildberger does (see JPS and NIV). Thus this short grammatical construction, *noun* + ליהוה, reveals its polysemy through these possible translations.

Verse 2 closes with a bicolon composed of two short cola without an introductory or a connecting waw; this gives a sense of rapidity and near identity to the two actions. The bicolon can be scanned as a long colon to produce a tricolon of 3:2:3 for all of v. 2 with long cola in terms of syllables.

> Yes, wrath for YHWH against all the nations
> and fury against all their armies.
> He has doomed them, he has given them to the slaughter.

This would also accentuate the rapid effect; the separation into two short cola, however, slows the pace and detaches the actions from each other. Different possible scansions testify to the polysemy and plurality of the poem just as do the various possible translations for a given word or phrase. In addition, this is an example of how printing the text, presenting it on the page, affects our reading of the poem (see above, pp. 19-20).

'Has doomed' and 'has given' are in the English perfect tense, which indicates a past action with effects continuing into the present. I can translate using the present, 'he dooms them, he gives them to the slaughter', that would increase the vividness and immediacy of the acts. I employ the perfect to give a narrative quality to this scene in vv. 2-4: wrath leads to doom and slaughter, which are the actions that result in the human corpses and the incredible effects on nature.

With Waltke and O'Connor, I take the Hebrew 'perfect' conjugation, which I will refer to as the *qatal* form,[3] as marking perfectivity, that is, it presents the action of the verb as a whole, as a complete act, and not as a process, as an act in its stages. The two verbs in *qatal* denote the actions of dooming and giving and not the processes involved; therefore, I prefer the English perfect for my translation of these two verbs.

The two cola of v. 3a-b, in contrast to 2c-d, both begin with waw attached to the noun subjects: '*and* their slain... *and* their corpses'. This

---

3. Waltke and O'Connor 1990: 455-86. 'Perfect' is the traditional term for the conjugation that is also called the perfective, the suffix, the *qtl* or the *qātal* conjugation. I refer to the *waw* + suffix conjugation as the *weqatal* form (Waltke and O'Connor 1990: 519-42).

changes the rhythm, slows the rapidity of the preceding divine action and presents, with deliberation, the repulsive results of those actions. Verse 3b uses a different syntax than 3a and thereby focuses both on the corpses and on their prevalent fetid odor; the varied syntax is in part due to the need to begin the colon with 'and their corpses' rather than 'and the odor of their corpses'. The image of the rising odor involves a third sense: we hear, see and smell.

The two verbs are 'imperfect', *yiqtol*, in my study,[4] that, with Waltke and O'Connor, is the conjugation denoting imperfectivity—that is, it describes 'a *process* (rather than an event). Imperfectivity directs attention to the internal distinctions of various separate phases making up the situation' (1990: 480). The other major value of the conjugation is to signify a dependent situation whether the dependence is on the speaker, the subject or something else (Waltke and O'Connor 1990: 502). I take imperfectivity as the dominant value in this bicolon (3a-b) that is describing the results of YHWH's acts in the passive voice. YHWH himself does not act here as he did in the preceding. 'Are thrown out' and 'goes up' can be rendered 'are being thrown out' and 'is rising' to accentuate the sense of the process, of the separate phases of the action. I repeat that, as with תשמע and כי, the choice of tense is made for an English translation; the Hebrew verbs express process, not just one tense.

Poetic Style: Parallelism. Throughout the poem the poet employs the resources of parallelism, both its regularity and its variety, to present the scenes in an impressionistic mode that gains much of its strength from piling one image on another while, at the same time, advancing the tableau. Most of the parallels in 1a-3b are between synonyms, such as peoples and nations, earth and world, and slain and corpses, rather than between pairs of different entities. The latter is established in 3c-d where 'mountains' and 'heavens' are paralleled in a type of merismus. At this point, the poet has a God's-eye point of view that first encompasses all the earth and then the heavens. The transition of the point of view from earth to heaven is marked imagistically by the ascent of the

---

4.   Waltke and O'Connor 1990: 455-78, 496-506. 'Imperfect' is the traditional term for the conjugation that is also called the non-perfective, the prefix, the *yqtl* or the *yiqtôl* conjugation. I refer to the *waw* + prefix conjugation form, the '*waw* conversive', as *wayyiqtol* and as *weyiqtol* when there is no 'conversion'.

corpses' fetid odor. As we picture it going up, the poet takes us up the mountains and to the heavens.

An Encyclopedic Quality

> Approach, O Nations, to hear!
> O Peoples, pay attention!
> Let the earth and all that fills it hear,
> the world and all that springs from it.

All humanity and the entire earth are called to hear the poet and to view the scenes of devastation. This refers us to similar calls in Isaiah, for example, 28.23, 33.13, and summonses to attend to YHWH's acts of judgment and restoration, for example, 41.1, 21-22; 43.9 and 49.1. The parallels place 34–35 solidly within Isaiah. Mathews (1995: 35-51) discusses the form-critical studies of the opening that attempt to fit it into a particular genre: a 'simple call to attention' (36), a 'summons to witness' in a prophetic lawsuit setting (37-40) and a 'summons to receive instruction' (41-42). I do not pursue this mode of analysis for it is too atomistic and treats the opening of the poem as though it were an entity separate from the rest of the poem. The call is the introduction to the poem and the parallels in the other parts of Isaiah are treated as intertextual allusions. In this digression I want to focus on this group of calls and summonses as an example of what I term Isaiah's encyclopedic quality. I note the other parallels but I do not attempt a developed reading of all of them and of all their details that can have a direct or indirect bearing on our poem. This is in line with my expansive mode of reading that can note and display possibilities without having to argue for or against a particular application (see above, pp. 23-24).

As noted previously, Isaiah's vision attempts to be all-embracing in both its content and its form. Isaiah envisions and at points addresses the entire world and all that lives in it, both human and animal. He speaks of and describes good and evil, peace and violence, destruction and restoration, fantastic dreams and nightmarish horror. He employs a wide variety of poetic forms to convey this rich content. In most studies of Isaiah, especially those with a form-critical bent, this varied style, these changes in form, are used to divide the book into separate sources and redactional levels on the assumption that a different style indicates different authorship and time of composition. However, I take the varied style as the formal counterpart of the thematic diversity and all-inclusiveness. This is an aspect of the play between regularity and variety. To put it simply, Isaiah wants to say as much as possible in as many ways as possible.

The vision opens in Isaiah 1 with a call for the heavens and the earth to hear; no direct object of attention is given but there is a motivating clause followed by a quotation.

> Hear, O heavens! and give ear, O earth! for YHWH speaks:
> 'Children I rear and bring up, but they rebel against me'.

In 1.10 humans, not nature, are addressed using the same verbs as in 1.2 and YHWH is again quoted; however, in this instance there are direct objects but no motivating clause.

> Hear the word of YHWH, you rulers of Sodom!
> Give ear to the teaching of our God, you people of Gomorrah!
> 'What to me is the multitude of your sacrifices?' says YHWH.

In this short space in his first chapter, the poet presents a fine example of regularity and diversity. Verse 18 of the same chapter is yet another way to summon listeners. There are no explicit addressees or direct objects; the call itself is a quotation of YHWH and a motivating clause is placed at the end of v. 20: 'for the mouth of YHWH speaks'.

> 'Come now, let us argue it out', says YHWH,
> 'Though your sins are like scarlet, they can be as white as snow'.

In 6.9, in a quotation within a quotation, the people paradoxically are called to pay attention so that they will not learn anything.[5]

> And he [YHWH] said [to the prophet], 'Go and say to this people:
> "Hear carefully but don't understand; look closely but don't know"'.

The poet can vary a call by expanding one or more of its parts, by using synonyms and new terminology and by changing the order of repeated terms. In the following example from 18.3-4, the prophet uses the verbs 'to hear' and 'to look' from 6.9 (but in reverse order), and the pair 'world–earth' that occurs, in reverse order, in 34.1.

> All you inhabitants of the world, you who dwell on the earth,
> When a standard is raised on the mountains, Look!
> When a trumpet is sounded, Hear!
> For thus YHWH says to me: 'I quietly gaze from my dwelling like the
>   glowing heat of the sun, like a cloud of dew in harvest heat'.

In 28.23, there are four imperatives; the second and fourth are the same:

---

5. See 8.9-10 and 29.9 for similar paradoxical calls.

'Give ear and hear my voice; pay attention and hear my words'. 'Pay attention', הקשיבו, occurs in 34.1. At 33.13, the contrast of near and far is introduced: 'Hear, you who are far, what I have done; know, you who are near, my might'. 'To be near', קרב, is the verb underlying the imperative, 'approach' or 'come near', in 34.1. 'Approach me! Hear this!' (48.16).

The following are further illustrations of the possible variations including word-play on near and far.

> Be silent before me, O coastlands! Let the peoples renew their strength!
> Let them approach, then let them speak. Let us draw near [נקרבה]
> together to settle this (41.1).

> Assemble and come, draw together, O survivors of the nations! (45.20).

> Hear me, O house of Jacob, all you remnant of the house of Israel!
> (46.3).

> Hear me, O hard-hearted, you who are far from deliverance! (46.12).

> Hear me, O coastlands! Pay attention, O peoples from afar! (49.1).

> Hear the word of YHWH, you who tremble at his word! (66.5).

This is a small sampling of the many variations on the call to hear in Isaiah (see above, p. 28, for the grammatical construction of 34.1a). The diversity could readily be increased by including calls to see using the particle 'Look', הנה, with a participle or *yiqtol* verb (3.1; 5.26; 54.11) and by all the calls to wail (14.31; 23.1), to hide (2.10; 26.20), to remember (44.21) and not to remember (43.18), to not fear (7.4; 37.6; 41.10; 54.4), to awake or rouse oneself (51.9, 17; 52.1), and so on.

To pursue this diversity at length would, therefore, take us into the entirety of the book of Isaiah and involve us in depth in the questions of who is speaking to whom, who is quoting whom, and so on. The examples do, however, underline the fact that the call in 34.1 and the poem that it introduces are an integral part of Isaiah, and that they exemplify the play between regularity and variety by illustrating, in different ways, Isaiah's encyclopedic quality that is the formal aspect of his drive to be all-inclusive.

Wrath and Doom. Against the global backdrop, the poet moves to a scene of divine wrath, doom and slaughter. Besides the references to other passages in Isaiah such as chs. 13, 57.15b-19 and 63.1-6, I could multiply biblical texts invoked by the terms and images but limit myself to noting that doom, the ban or dedication of holy war signified by the Hebrew root חרם, alludes to the militaristic and violent themes of the exodus and conquest of the land, particularly as expressed in Exodus 15 and Joshua.[6] Watts intones these themes and passages in his discussion of YHWH's imperial right to wrath which takes on a particular expression in 'his right to apply *the ban* to any one of [the nations]' (1987: 9; his emphasis). In Joshua, the ban—that is, utter or total destruction (see NIV and NRSV for these translations)—is applied to Sihon and Og (Josh. 2.10), Jericho (6.17, 21), Ai (8.26) and all the nations of Canaan (10.1 and 40). The ban can be executed 'by the edge of the sword' (Josh. 6.21; 8.26 and 10.28); this connects with the appearance of YHWH's sword in Isa. 34.5. I will trace the poet's presentation and treatment of these themes of wrath, doom and conquest of the land in the continuing reading.

YHWH. YHWH and his role are the final topic to be discussed in reference to these opening verses, 1a-3b. The poet proclaims, in v. 2, that YHWH's fury has turned against the nations. Unless, by a grammatical stretch, we understand the subject of the verbs in 2c-d to be an impersonal 'it' with a combined wrath and fury as the antecedent, the poet describes YHWH's specific actions of total destruction and handing over to slaughter. However, following this, YHWH is increasingly relegated to a passive role in most of the poem, a process that I will detail in the analysis. Verse 3a-b describes the results of the destruction with a passive verb—'their slain are thrown out', not 'YHWH casts out their slain'—and with an active verb—'goes up'—whose subject is 'their stench'.

The absence of any motive for the divine rage or for the countering joy and restoration is a striking feature of the poem. The poet describes events and resulting states with little space given to divine reasons or motives. This accords with the poet's increasing relegation of YHWH to the background of the poem, despite his consistent use of the proper

---

6.   See Lust 1989: 285-86 for discussion of the root חרם. He distinguishes two different meanings for it in 34.2 (total annihilation) and 34.5 (dedicated or devoted to YHWH either for service or for destruction). He claims that v. 5 represents the older use of the term and that this fits with the fact that the verse is in the oldest part of ch. 34, i.e. the oracle against Edom in vv. 5-6; v. 2 represents a later meaning found in a later section of the poem, i.e. the oracle against the nations found in vv. 2-3 (4) and 7.

name YHWH (34.2, 6 [*bis*], 8, 16; 35.2, 10). As I will soon explain in greater depth, my choice of terminology to this point such as nightmare, wrath and destruction rather than the more usual judgment, particularly in phrases such as 'Yahweh's judgment on the nations and on Edom', reflects this view. This is a poem about death, destruction and the resultant world, and the contrasting restoration, life and return—not a poem about YHWH's explicit acts of judgment and salvation. Let us read on.

34.3c-4

3c The mountains melt with their blood
4a   and all the armies of the heavens rot;[7]
b   The heavens roll up like a scroll,
c   and all their armies wither
d   Like leaves wither from the vine,
        like [a leaf] withering from the fig tree.

The three bicola form a tight unit in terms of both poetic structure and content. The two bicola in 3c-4c form a four-part section bound by the waws at the start of each colon. The first three cola are introduced by three *weqatal* verbs that, in content, continue the horrific description from 3a-b and that, in form, allow the poet to vary his style by changing verb forms. Before the three *weqatal* verbs, 2c-d contains two *qatal* forms and 3a-b contains two *yiqtol* forms. The three *weqatal* verbs, all niphal plurals, add assonance to the other features binding the section: וְנָמַסּוּ ,וְנָמַקּוּ and וְנָגֹלּוּ.[8] The poet closes 3c-4c by shifting to a singular qal *yiqtol* form (יִבּוֹל) placed at the end of the final colon; the poet has to shift verb forms to place the verb here since a *weqatal* can occur only at the beginning of a line. This verb יִבּוֹל thus both concludes 3c-4c and introduces the two similes in the final bicolon (4d-e) that employ the infinitive construct and feminine participle of the root of נבל—יבול, to

---

7.   In place of the Hebrew verb for 'they rot', נמקו, 1QIsaᵃ reads יתבקעו ו והעמקים: 'and the valleys break open and...' See Watts 1987: 5 and Wildberger 1982: 1326 for discussion. Wildberger suggests that this is a scribal expansion made on the basis of Mic. 1.4: 'The mountains melt beneath him and the valleys break open'. Mountain and valley are a pair in Isa. 40.4. Passages such as those in Mic. 1.4 and Isa. 40.4 are alluded to by the opening of our poem; 1QIsaᵃ is making the allusion literally obvious.

8.   See GKC 67t for the unusual niphal in *ô*; the *ô* vowel balances the following יבול. The poet chooses his words as much for poetic effect as to follow the rules of Hebrew grammar.

wither.[9] To underline the possibilities of variation amid identity, the poet uses three forms of the same root in three connected cola.

The use, and therefore the translation, of the verbal system in Hebrew poetry is an area of debate. 'The most remarkable area of disagreement is an apparently free alternation of Qatal, Yiqtol and W^eqatal forms in poetry' (Niccacci 1997: 91). Hebrew prose reveals a much tighter use of the verb forms, especially since they usually occur in set sequences.

Waltke and O'Connor discuss, at some length, the history and present status of the Hebrew verbal system, particularly the thorny issue of whether *weqatal* and *wayyiqtol* forms entail a change in the aspect of the verb, that is, whether a *weqatal* can take on the imperfective aspect otherwise reserved for *yiqtol*, and *wayyiqtol* take on the perfective aspect of *qatal*.[10] They argue for this change in aspect, traditionally called *waw-consecutive* or *waw-conversive*. In relation to *weqatal*, they distinguish between *waw-relative* that can involve such a shift because the verbal action is relative to or dependent on the preceding situation, and *waw-copulative* that does not involve the shift because the action is not relative to the preceding (1990: 519-20). (The only *wayyiqtol* form in the poem is in 34.15a; see below, p. 85.)

This produces two different readings and translations for our passage. If we see 3c as *waw-copulative*, then this colon begins a comparatively new description of the wrath and its effects. This is reflected in my presentation and analysis above, in which vv. 3c-4e are marked out as a lexia. If we see 3c as *waw-relative*, then the colon is closely connected with the preceding and the relation expressed in a slightly different translation and presentation that does not separate v. 3a-b from 3c-4e:

9.   The participle is feminine, probably through attraction to the following feminine noun 'fig tree' that can also mean the fruit 'fig' as in Num. 13.23 and Jer. 24.1-8. The assumed noun, represented by (a leaf) in the translation, can be (a fig) or (fruit); NRSV renders 'or fruit withering on a fig tree' (see JPS). The feminine form may be influenced by the similar phrase in 1.30. The people are 'like an oak whose leaves are withering'; literally the phrase is 'an oak withering [נבלת] as to its leaves' (see GKC 116i and Waltke and O'Connor 1990: 617 for discussion of the grammatical construction). 'Oak' is a feminine noun and the participle agrees in gender. In ch. 34, the feminine form produces a colon, v. 4e, composed of two feminine forms that contrasts with v. 4d that is composed of an infinitive and two masculine forms.

10.   Their general treatment is on pp. 455-78. 'Waw + Suffix Conjugation' is discussed on pp. 519-42 and 'Waw + Prefix Conjugation' on pp. 543-63.

> Their slain are thrown out
>> and their corpses: their stench goes up.
> The mountains melt with their blood
>> and all the armies of the heavens rot...

However, in both of these I translate the verbs with English present tenses because of the environment, two preceding *yiqtol*s and one following, and to emphasize the immediacy of the images of melting, rotting and rolling up.

In this reading of Isaiah 34–35, I approach the issue on the assumption that the poet is employing the complexity and variety of the Hebrew verbal system and syntax to increase diversity of both words and structure and to place the poem and its scenes in a general time and aspect that is not clearly or exclusively perfective or imperfective, or past, present or future. Throughout the poem, the poet exploits the richness of Hebrew terminology, grammar and syntax for poetic effect. Therefore my translations of the varying verb forms throughout the poem are made for both grammatical and poetic reasons.

The three bicola in 3c-4e continue the description of the effects of YHWH's wrath; 'their blood' connects with the dead corpses of 2c-d. Note that it is effects that are described and not the direct action of YHWH. For a contrast to clarify the point, I cite 13.11-13 that foregrounds the divine 'I'.

> I punish the world for its evil and the wicked for their sin;
> I bring the pride of the arrogant to an end and I lay low the hubris of
>> tyrants.
> I make humans rarer than pure gold and mortals than gold of Ophir.
> Therefore I make the heavens shake and the earth is torn from its place
> Because of the rage of YHWH of hosts in the day of his blazing anger.

This is not to make a general claim that it is only in ch. 34–35 that the poet downplays the role of YHWH, but it does stress the need to read a given text of Isaiah closely, and not to assume automatically that YHWH is always the major actor if he is named or assume that we already know what the text is saying.[11]

---

11. For example, in a common interpretive move, Wildberger (1982: 1341) notes the absence of any explicit motivation for the divine fury but then cancels the effect of the comment on his reading. To put it somewhat simplistically, he knows what the text says even though it doesn't actually say it: 'Yahweh is filled with anger and fury that now break loose. Yahweh certainly has reason to be angry, but the writer says nothing about it in some contrast to 24,1ff. For him the weight of guilt is so heavy that he would consider it superfluous to say anything about it.'

The effects of the divine fury now extend beyond humanity to all nature represented by the merismus of the mountains and the heavens. The poet is varying his treatment of the parallel pair—heavens and earth—that appear in that order, for example, in 1.2, 37.16, 42.5, 65.17 and 66.1, and in the reverse order in 40.22 and 48.13. 'I made the earth...my hands stretched out the heavens' (45.12). He begins with 'earth' in 34.1 and holds the contrasting 'heavens' until v. 4 where it stands in antithesis with 'mountains', a synecdoche for earth.

The armies of both the nations and the heavens are devastated (see 13.2-5). The military imagery is stressed since the term 'army', צָבָא, is used three times (in 2b, 4a and 4c). The poet takes the phrase 'the armies of the heavens' of 4a and employs the two parts, in reverse order, in 4b-c: the heavens roll up and their armies wither. Blood, occurring in 3c, is an expected image because of the preceding slaughter and it is intensified through the added imagery of melting and rotting. Rotting, in turn, accords with the rising stench of corpses.

The heavens rolling up contrasts with the creator God's ability to 'stretch out the heavens like a curtain and to spread them like a tent to dwell in' (40.22). In addition to having contrasting effects on the heavens, the antithesis of the passive act of the rolling up of the heavens and God's active stretching them out underlines the fact that our poet is describing the effect of the divine wrath on humanity and nature while saying a minimal amount about YHWH's actual actions and possible motives. Corpses are cast out, mountains melt and the heavens roll up: these are passive statements (using hophal and niphal stems) that do not indicate the agent who is performing the actions. YHWH, as an active force, is moved into the background in the poem.

'Roll up like a scroll': the only other occurrence in Isaiah of the verb 'to roll up', גלל, is in 9.4, in the vivid image of garments rolled in blood being fed to the fire; both blood and fire are images in our poem. A scroll can be sealed for a future generation: 'Now, go, write it on a tablet before them and inscribe it in a scroll so that it may be for a future time as an everlasting witness' (30.8; see 8.16). It is something that both cannot be read and yet can be.

> The vision of all this has become to you like the words of a sealed scroll. If they give it to someone who knows how to read commanding, 'Read this', he says, 'I can't for it is sealed'. If the scroll is given to someone who doesn't know how to read commanding, 'Read this', he says, 'I don't know how to read' (29.11-12).

Is it not just a little while before Lebanon becomes farm land and farm land is thought of as a forest? On that day the deaf will hear the words of a scroll while from their deep gloom the blind will see (29.17-18).[12]

The blind and the deaf appear in the latter part of our poem, 35.5, where they are given sight and hearing amid another scene of the transformation of nature. Finally, the command to find and to read a scroll occurs in the enigmatic transition between the two parts of the poem; we will discuss the line, 34.16, in its context.

The heavenly armies wither or fade; withering is a notable image in Isaiah. The Israelites are 'like an oak whose foliage is withering' (1.30; see p. 38 n. 9); the earth and the world wither (24.4; see 34.1); the flower withers because of the divine breath/wind (40.7-8); and, similar to 1.30 and our poem, the people in their sin 'wither like foliage' (64.5). 'To wither', נבל, suggests a group of similar sounding words: נְבָלָה, foolishness (9.16; 32.6); נְבֵלָה, corpse (5.25; 26.19); נָבָל, fool (32.5-6); נֵבֶל, a jar that can fall and break (22.24; 30.14) and a harp that can be stilled (14.11); and נפל, to fall (14.12; 21.9).[13] Thus the Hebrew word and root for withering intone a wide variety of other concepts and images: corpses, falling, breaking, fool(ishness), silence, music and hope. 'Grass dries, a flower withers, but the word of our God lasts forever' (40.8). Listing such parallels stresses the polysemy of our poem and accords with my practice of reading in a fashion that proceeds by noting many parallels, alternative interpretations and scansions, and so on, and by not limiting myself to only those that support a specific reading or meaning (see above, pp. 23-24).

Poetic Style: Imagery. Until now I have spoken of images and imagery in relation to all of Isaiah as a vision and, in particular, to the images of our poem, for example, slaughter, corpses and stench. An image is a concrete, physical object, even including a person, that is described in the language of the text and that we, the readers, can visualize and

---

12. See 37.14 and 39.1 for references to a scroll in the everyday sense of an object containing a message.

13. 'In Isaiah they [*nābal, nāpal*] are also close in meaning, especially in this passage, since withering of leaves implies their falling; therefore, the passage employs "from" ' (Miscall 1992b: 56): 'leaves wither from the vine'. Indeed, RSV translates: 'All their host shall fall, as leaves fall from the vine, like leaves falling from the fig tree' (see NJB). This mirrors the earlier KJV: 'and all their host shall fall down, as the leaf falleth off from the vine, and a falling fig from the fig tree'.

imaginatively hear, touch, smell or taste. An image tends to the sensual and the imaginative, and a theme to the intellectual. For example, we see an ox and we think, dumb. An image is a particular object, for example, a tree or grass; imagery is a larger grouping of images, for example, vegetal imagery. As with many of the literary categories and distinctions employed in this study, I use image and theme with a garden variety understanding of them and of their contrast. They are helpful in discussing a reading of the poem, but they do not reflect hard-and-fast distinctions in the language of the poem.

Images occur throughout the book of Isaiah and, bound together in sets of imagery, serve to hold the disparate parts and themes of the vision together. Imagery is another fine illustration of the poet's drive to be all-inclusive. Isaiah does not offer just individual images, since he develops an image by looking at its different aspects and relations to other images, by giving many examples of it and by using an image or imagery in a variety of settings and with a variety of themes so that it can have different and even opposed meanings. As already commented on, fury and doom can be against the nations and therefore for Israel's benefit, or they can be turned against Israel himself. A tree can be an image of misery—'I am a dry tree' (56.3)—and of life—'the days of my people will be like the days of a tree' (65.22). Water can be life-sustaining—'I turn the wilderness into ponds and the dry land into springs of water' (41.18)—or destructive—'YHWH is now bringing up against them the mighty and massive waters of the River: the king of Assyria and his army!' (8.7). Throughout this analysis, I comment on specific images and phrases in the poem and their parallels within Isaiah; here I focus on trees, foliage, and so on—that is, vegetal imagery, and its importance for our poem and for the vision of Isaiah.

Vegetal imagery is first alluded to in the 'vineyard' and 'cucumber field' of 1.8 and then explicitly intoned at the close of ch. 1 in the reference to 'oaks', 'gardens' and 'an oak whose leaf withers' (1.29-30); the references are in a context of sin and punishment. It is last referred to in the 'gardens' of 65.3 and 66.17, the 'tree' and the 'straw' of 65.22 and 25 and the 'grass' of 66.14. 'Gardens' are in negative contexts while the others are in contexts speaking of life and peace. On the other hand, to be 'like Eden…like YHWH's garden' (51.3) is a powerful image of consolation. Within the book of Isaiah, vegetal imagery occurs in virtually every chapter with the characteristic balance or tension between regularity and diversity. A telling aspect of the diversity is the fact that the poet uses approximately 100 terms for plants, foliage, types of gardens, and so on, and that approximately one-half of these terms occur only once in the book of Isaiah and some of these, only once in the Hebrew Bible.

As part of the range of the imagery, Isaiah refers to the full process of planting, growth and harvesting; this is summarized in the following two passages.

> Although you plant plants for the Pleasant One [a fertility god] and set
>   out slips for a strange god,
> Although you make them grow on the day you plant them and make
>   them blossom on the very morning you sow them,
> The harvest disappears in a day of disease and incredible pain (17.10-11).

> He will provide rain for your seed with which you sow the ground and
> the grain, the produce of the ground, will be rich and nourishing. Your
> cattle will feed on that day in broad pastures; the oxen and the donkeys
> that till the ground will eat salted fodder that has been winnowed with
> shovel and fork (30.23-24).[14]

In our poem, plant imagery occurs in the central portion between the 'withering foliage' of 34.4 and the 'grass', 'reed' and 'rush' of 35.7. There are ten terms for plants and parts of plants—leaves, vine and fig tree (34.4); thorns, nettles, brambles and grass (34.13); crocus (35.1); and reed and rush (35.7). 'Grass', which is the only term repeated, occurs in 34.13 and 35.7. Further, 'thorns', סירים, 'nettles', קמוש, and 'brambles', חוח, occur only here in Isaiah. Finally, there is variety in the types of both domestic and wild plants, both the vine and the brambles. This plant imagery is an illustration of how the poem is an integral part of the book in terms of both content, the imagery itself, and form, the play between regularity and diversity.

A Fantastic Reading. As discussed in the introduction and commented on in the above analyses, I am employing at many points in my reading a set of terms and concepts that are quite different from those usually found in biblical studies, particularly in studies of Isaiah. Many of these terms are, directly or indirectly, taken and developed from the

---

14. Further examples occur in the Vineyard Song (5.1-7), the parable of the farmer (28.23-29), in the sign provided to Hezekiah (37.30-32) and in the promise of success in 55.10-11. 'Sprouting' or 'springing forth' is an image for the prophet's message that YHWH is doing something new. 'I am doing something new: right now it is sprouting, don't you perceive it?' (43.19; see 42.9 and 45.8).

contemporary study of fantastic literature, a literature that includes both fantasy and horror (see above, pp. 22-24). I turn now to discuss what some of these terms and concepts are, what their assumptions and implications are and how they affect this reading of a poem in the vision of Isaiah.

The first indication of the change occurs in the title of the monograph: *Isaiah 34–35: A Nightmare/A Dream*. The title is adapted from my article 'Isaiah: Dreams and Nightmares, Fantasy and Horror'. I quote from the essay to define the terms.

> I am using fantasy in the non-literary but positive sense of a dream or fairy tale in which the world is better than could ever be expected or hoped for in real life. In Isaiah's terms, God's bounty overflows in a surfeit of light (30.26), peace (2.4; 11.6-9) and prosperity. Horror is the opposite. It is the nightmare of violence and destruction (2.10-21), death and dearth (5.11-17), when God's wrath bursts forth and consumes all. 'The Light of Israel becomes Fire; his Holy One, Flame; he burns and devours his thorns and briers in a single day (10.17).'
>
> Somewhere in between the dream and the nightmare is waking life and the world we live in. It is a time and place for hope and fear (8.16-22; 30.18-33), hoping for the dream and fearing the nightmare (1997: 153).

The nightmare is analogous to Frye's category of the demonic epiphany.

> The dark tower and prison of endless pain, the city of dreadful night in the desert, or, with a more erudite irony, the *tour abolie*, the goal of the quest that isn't there...[a] blasted world of repulsiveness and idiocy, a world without pity and without hope (1957: 238-39).[15]

The terminological shift turns our focus to the poem itself and to the images and scenes that it presents. What Twitchell says about horror movies applies equally to both fantasy and horror in poetry. 'Stories don't carry horror; images do' (1985: 58). To this point in the poem the poet presents a cosmic scene of the divine rage that spends itself upon both humanity and the armies of the heavens. Earth is drenched in blood and the heavens fade away. It is as though YHWH of hosts/armies turns against his own forces that he has created (40.26) and that he has marshaled for cosmic battle.

---

15. Frye does not have a similar encapsulated statement describing a dream world, which would belong in his categories of comedy and romance, but the latter do have relevance to my ongoing discussion.

YHWH of armies is mustering an army for war.
They are coming from a far land, from the ends of the heavens,
YHWH and his furious forces, to destroy the entire earth (13.4-5).

In our poem, the poet paints the gruesome scene in vivid and direct terms; he closes with three similes: 'like a scroll', 'like leaves wither' and 'like [a leaf] withering'. These are the only similes in the first part of our poem and the only group of similes in the entire poem. The other two similes, 'like the crocus' and 'like deer', occur in the second part of the poem in separate contexts (35.1, 6).[16] In the context of 34.4 the similes increase the impact of the remarkable images and, at the same time, draw our attention to the lack of similar similes in the poem. The lack, in its own way, adds to the vividness of the depicted scenes including the creatures—both animal and human—that inhabit them. The poet describes precisely what is there; he does not say that it is like something else.

For contrast, I cite 1.8 whose imagery of an isolated and besieged city is narrated in more 'literal' fashion in the story of Sennacherib's siege of Jerusalem in chs. 36–37.

And daughter Zion is left
like a booth in a vineyard,
like a lodge in a cucumber field,
like a besieged city.[17]

In the Bible, vine and fig tree are an image of prosperity in the land (Deut. 8.8). 'Judah and Israel dwelt in security, each under their own vine and fig tree' (1 Kgs 5.5; see Mic. 4.4; Zech. 3.10). And they are, at the same time, an image of destruction when they are removed (Ps. 105.33). 'They [a distant nation] will consume your flocks and your

16. The five similes are all composed of the comparative particle 'like' (כ) attached to a single word, whether a noun, infinitive or participle; only the second simile is comprised of a phrase, a construct chain: 'like-the-withering-of-leaves'.

17. This is NRSV (see NIV and NJB); other translations are similar, e.g. JPS, 'like a city beleaguered' (see REB), and NAB, 'like a city blockaded'. Watts (1985: 14), however, renders 'like a fortified city' and notes that 'Judean kings did build up fortified border cities throughout their history. Such a city would in fact be an outpost to watch or guard the border. It could easily be overrun or by-passed in an attack'. Others, such as Kaiser and Wildberger, propose major emendations. Kaiser (1983: 17) renders '<like a refuge in the sheepfold>', and the < > indicate the conjectural nature of the proposal. Wildberger (1972: 18-19) translates 'wie ein Eselfüllen "im Pferch" ' ('as a donkey-colt in a pen') and the quotation marks indicate the conjectural nature of the reading.

herds; they will consume your vine and your fig tree' (Jer. 5.17). The double value of the image is contained in the Assyrian king's ironic promise to take the people to a new land where they can eat from their own vine and fig tree: prosperity in exile (Isa. 36.16 = 2 Kgs 18.31)! Finally, let us not forget Adam and Eve who clothe themselves with fig leaves before their encounter with God and their eventual exile from the garden (Gen. 3.7; see Miscall 1992b: 50).

Thus these grim images of the heavens rolling up, a closed scroll and the withering and desiccation of vine and fig tree contain memories and traces of creation, hope and prosperity. We encountered an analogous situation with the ban, the total doom, of v. 2 that recalls Joshua and the conquest of the land. The nightmare, the gore and the devastation, is the manifest meaning of the vision, while the dream, the hope for abundant life in one's land, is the latent meaning that can disturb and unsettle the nightmare.

This is Freudian terminology drawn from his seminal work *The Interpretation of Dreams*.[18] For Freud the manifest content of a dream is what we explicitly remember of the dream while the latent content is the unconscious thoughts that lie underneath the dream and that form the true object of dream interpretation. For Freud all dreams are wish-fulfilments, that is, the latent, unconscious thoughts expressing themselves in an actual, manifest dream are working out the fulfilment of a wish or desire of the dreamer. Thus even 'distressing dreams and anxiety-dreams, when they have been interpreted, may turn out to be fulfilments of wishes' (1965: 168). Over and above the question of whether this is a valid theory for dream interpretation,[19] I find the notion of manifest and latent meanings for one dream or one text

18. This was first published in 1900 and revised seven times between 1909 and 1930. Consult Freud 1965: 168, 311-18, 340 and 544-45 for clear, succinct statements of Freud's theory.

19. Dreams are texts that exist in both oral and written form and, as any other text, are subject to reading and interpretation by the dreamer and by anyone else who learns of the dream. Debating whether a particular approach or theory is valid is far beyond the scope of this monograph. I note that Freud's demonstration that a nightmare can be a wish-fulfilment is dependent on its first having been interpreted. Pardon the pun, but this is a self-fulfilling theory. On the other hand, in the interpretive gymnastics that Freud employs to show what wishes dreams are fulfilling, he teaches us a great deal about the possibilities and the pitfalls of reading and interpretation and of the claims that they make for themselves. I am employing one of these possibilities—the distinction of manifest and latent content—in this study.

intriguing, particularly when it allows us to speak, paradoxically, of a nightmare being disturbed by the positive thoughts and images of wishes and dreams.

In our poem this means that we unsettle a reading or interpretation that claims to see the opening verses solely in the negative terms of slaughter and destruction and that would simply deny the relevance of any of the positive connotations of terms and images. However, in my expansive mode of reading, I don't deny the relevance of such conno-tations and much of what I have been detailing and will continue to detail is part of this bivalent or multivalent reading that sees the night-mare and the dream, fantasy and horror, the positive and the negative, inextricably intertwined and imbricated. This is my main appropriation of the notion, in the study of the fantastic, of hesitation or oscillation. In reading the poem, I often find myself caught or suspended between alternative readings of the same text, between different interpretations of the same image or scene, especially when the alternatives and differ-ences stand in sharp contrast, if not outright contradiction.

This fantastic way of reading, and fantastic in both critical and popu-lar understandings of the term, will be deepened and expanded in the following pages, and I will then address the possibility that this latent meaning, this message of hope and prosperity, applies to Israel. That is, perhaps we are not caught between mutually exclusive readings and interpretations but are reading a two-pronged message: manifest judg-ment for the nations and latent victory for Israel (see below, p. 55).

34.5-7

5   Yes, my sword drank its fill in the heavens![20]
      Now it comes down on Edom,
          yes, on my doomed people, for judgment.
6   A sword for YHWH:
          it is filled with blood,
          it is gorged with fat,
      With the blood of lambs and goats,
          with the fat of the innards of rams.[21]

20. I read this line as a colon standing on its own, emphasizing the suddenness of the divine proclamation. This is similar to JPS: 'For my sword shall be drunk in the sky' (see NJB and REB); NRSV (and NAB) connects it more closely with the fol-lowing colon: 'When my sword has drunk its fill in the heavens, lo, it will descend upon Edom'.

21. The poet ties this bicolon to the preceding by the repetition of מֵחֵלֶב, 'with

Yes, a sacrifice for YHWH in Bozrah,
>   and a great slaughter in the land of Edom.[22]
7   Wild oxen go down with them,
>   and young bulls with bulls;
Their land drinks its fill of blood,[23]
>   and their dust is gorged with fat.[24]

'Drank its fill': I read this as an intransitive piel with intensive effect.[25]
1QIsa[a] and the Targum read 'is seen', תראה, that is adopted by both
Watts and Wildberger. 'For my sword appears in heaven' (REB). Even
though I retain the MT, I think that the context, both immediate (הנה:
'behold!' in v. 5b) and removed ('see YHWH's glory' in 35.2), supports
the allusive presence of 'see', a presence that 1QIsa[a] makes explicit.[26] I
reiterate that I approach text-critical issues as much more a matter of
alternate readings, including making an allusion concrete as here, than a
matter of establishing the original reading, the Urtext.

The root to 'water' and 'drench', רוה, occurs in positive settings in
Isaiah. Rain and snow come down from heaven to *water* the earth and
make it flourish (55.10); the people can be like a *well-watered* garden if
they observe the proper fast (58.11). What follows in 34.6-15 depicts
anything but a well-watered garden. However, this horrific description,
in all its violence and negativity, is accompanied by brief flashes of
scenes of peace and prosperity. The manifest nightmare covers a latent
dream; the burning waste displaces Eden, YHWH's garden (51.3).

'My sword' and 'my doomed people': with most translations, I keep
the first person singular suffix of MT. Wildberger (1982: 1326-27), with
others, proposes to emend these to 'his sword' and 'his ban', חרבו and

the fat'.

22. The waw on 6g can be understood as an emphatic as in 5c: 'even a great
slaughter ... ' The bicolon is balanced by the assonance of זֶבַח, sacrifice, and טֶבַח,
slaughter, that occur at the beginning of their respective cola. טֶבַח occurs first in
v. 2d.

23. Note that 'blood' occurs four times in the first seven verses: 3c, 6a, 6c and
7c.

24. This is the third occurrence of 'with fat', מֵחֵלֶב, 6c, 6e and 7d.

25. See GKC 52k; there is a parallel in Isa. 51.3. The LXX and the Latin read the
verb as a qal.

26. There is a slight literal similarity between רוה, to drink, and ראה, to see, but
without the contextual allusions. I don't think that the similarity in itself is enough
to explain the change. In 4a, 1QIsa[a] has a textual change that introduces 'the valleys break open' into the text to literalize the allusion to the pair 'mountains and
valleys'; see p. 37 n. 7.

חרמו, or 'sword of YHWH' and 'ban of YHWH', חרב יהוה and חרם יהוה, suggesting that the suffix of MT חרבי and חרמי might be an abbreviation for יהוה. There is no textual evidence for the emendation and Wildberger's reasoning in support of it can work two ways. 'The suffix on חרבי cannot be correct since Yahweh is spoken of only in the 3rd pers. in the pericope' (1326); however, the fact that YHWH is spoken of only in the third person in the poem can highlight the impact of this 'interruption' by YHWH. I will return to this topic in later general comments on these verses.

'My doomed people' is literally 'people of my ban', עם חרמי, and is generally taken to mean 'the people that I've devoted to destruction'. There is a similar construction in Isa. 10.6 where Israel is referred to as 'people of my anger', עם עברתי, that is, a people who have angered YHWH and are now to suffer the effects of that anger; in 1 Kgs 20.42, YHWH refers to Ben-hadad as 'the man that I've devoted to destruction', איש חרמי.[27] I render the waw attached to the prepositional phrase (ועל...) that introduces 'my doomed people' as emphatic—'yes, on my doomed people' rather than 'and on my...' I will later discuss the question of whether 'Edom' and 'my doomed people' are the same or two different objects for the sword.

'Judgment', מִשְׁפָּט, is a frequent term in Isaiah. It can mean justice in the general sense that society, especially as represented in the powers of government and the courts, accord its members fair and equitable treatment (1.17; 10.2; 41.1-4). It often occurs in parallel with 'righteousness', צֶדֶק and צְדָקָה, to produce the phrase 'justice and righteousness' that expresses the ideal of a just and orderly society, whether of a nation or of the entire world (1.21, 27; 5.7; 9.6; 33.5; 56.1). In a limited number of cases it can mean judgment in the sense of a trial, usually with the implication that the accused will be found guilty.

> YHWH rises to argue his case (רִיב); he stands to judge (דִין) peoples.
> YHWH enters into judgment (מִשְׁפָּט) with the elders of his people and
> their princes:
> 'It is you who have devoured the vineyard; the spoil of the poor is in
> your houses. What do you mean by crushing my people, by grinding the
> face of the poor?' (3.13-15).[28]

---

27. In Lev. 27.21, a field released at the time of jubilee is a field holy to YHWH that is to be devoted to him; it is a שׂדה חרם that only a priest can use.

28. See 4.4; 28.6; 41.1; 54.17.

In 34.5 it is usually translated 'judgment' in a sense that combines the three meanings of the trial, the guilty verdict and the carrying out of the sentence. The violent and bloody context requires this type of understanding, but the sense of justice, of fairness, lingers in the background; I will say more about this shortly. Some translations stress the sense of punishment, the execution of the sentence.

> My sword…now falls on Edom,
> On the people vowed to destruction,
> To punish them (NJB).

JPS is similar:

> My sword…shall come down upon Edom,
> Upon the people I have doomed,
> to wreak judgment.

NRSV (see REB) connects it directly with the word 'doom'.

> My sword…will descend upon Edom,
> upon the people I have doomed to judgment.

'Drank its fill' is a *qatal* while 'comes down' is a *yiqtol* introduced by הנה, an emphatic particle which draws attention to the action. I translate in a narrative vein; the sword has done its work in the heavens and now comes to earth. This produces an overall movement to this point: the poet opens on earth, moves to the heavens and now returns to earth where he will remain for the rest of the poem.

Edom is a neighboring country, southeast of Judah and the Dead Sea. Despite being the descendant of Esau, Jacob's twin, Edom is a frequent foe of Israel and Judah in the Hebrew Bible and is the object of judgmental prophecies, for example, Num. 24.18; Jer. 49.7-22; Ezek. 35.1-15 and Amos 1.11-12. Edom does not play a significant role in Isaiah. It is listed with Moab and Ammon as an enemy in 11.14; its byname, Seir, appears in 21.11 as a place name; and it, combined with its capital, Bozrah, are the point of departure for YHWH's march in 63.1-6.

YHWH speaks in 34.5; he presents his sword as it descends to earth for judgment. The poet reasserts his voice in v. 6 and stresses YHWH's possession of a sword in parallel with his wrath (v. 2a). The poet sidesteps any question of judgment (or justice) and returns to the vivid imagery of blood and slaughter. I break the opening of v. 6 into a tricolon containing three short cola; the first announces the subject of

the tricolon and the next two describe its gory condition. The three cola
are not joined with waws and are framed by the assonance of חֶרֶב and
מֵחֵלֶב, the first and last terms.

As with 'wrath for YHWH' in v. 2, this second occurrence of the
phrase '*noun* + ליהוה' is followed by two *qatals*.[29] We see the results of
the sacrifice and not the process, the acts of slaughter. Verse 6d-e, two
noun clauses, details the gore that bloats the sword. The noun clauses
repeat 'blood' and 'fat', employ only one conjunction and name three
types of domestic animals that are all suitable for sacrifice. To vary the
style, the poet balances the first two animals with a graphic phrase, 'the
innards of rams'. In English idiom, the bicolon depicts the sword
covered with blood and guts.

These animals are also metaphors for human leaders in other parts of
the Hebrew Bible (Ezek. 39.17-20).[30] The manifest talk of animal
slaughter contains hints of a latent and matching human bloodbath that
lingers somewhere behind or beneath this text. The human impact was
introduced directly in vv. 2-3 when YHWH handed the nations over 'to
the slaughter' and in the descent of the sword on the doomed people in
v. 5. However, unlike most commentaries, I am not trying to read the
description in 34.6-15 as a transparent metaphor for the human realm
that is devastated by the sword. In accord with my comments on the
relative paucity of similes and other obvious figures of speech, I draw
attention to the 'literal' and vivid style of the poet. As I said above, the
poet depicts what is there—the blood and guts of dead animals—not
something else that they are like.

'Yes', at the start of 6e, reflects polyvalent כי. The bicolon is an
emphatic conclusion to and an explanation of the preceding; it both
asserts and clarifies that this is a sacrifice and a slaughter. The latter
pair emphasize the carnage. The waw at the start of 6f can be emphatic:
'even a great slaughter'. 'A sacrifice for YHWH' is the third occurrence
of the phrase '*noun* + ליהוה'. Its syntax is similar to that in 2a-b, two

---

29. This is not an exact parallel since the poet varies his syntax. 'Wrath for
YHWH' is followed by a prepositional phrase and than a parallel clause for 'his
fury'; in v. 6 the verbal clauses immediately follow 'a sword for YHWH' and then
come the noun clauses.

30. For 'goats' see Isa. 14.9; Jer. 50.8 and Zech. 10.3; for 'rams' see Exod.
15.15; 2 Kgs 24.15 and Ezek. 32.21. See Watson 1984: 311 for a discussion of this
figure of speech.

parallel clauses, but unlike the first two uses of the phrase, this is followed by two *weqatal*s and a final *yiqtol*.[31] This is the same construction as in 3c-4a. I translate all three verbs with a present tense in
English that connotes both the process of going down and becoming
soaked and the final condition.

'In Bozrah' and 'in Edom' are usually interpreted as meaning that
this is a sacrifice of Edomites, a judgment on Edom. However, to this
point in the poem, Edom and Bozrah are the earthly site of the gory
sacrifice which involves the Edomites among all the other nations
(including the Israelites?). I connect this with Isa. 63.1-6 where YHWH
is coming from Edom and Bozrah after a bloody episode of vengeance,
redemption and fury against peoples, not just the Edomites; I cite the
full text below on p. 62. In 34.5-9, the poet is vague on the issue of
whether YHWH remains in Edom or moves on to Israel and Zion.

Verse 7 continues the list of animals, including the allusion to human
leaders[32] from v. 6; however, only 'young bulls', פָּרִים, are proper for
sacrifice. The animals are the immediate antecedents of 'with *them*' and
of '*their* land and dust'; the nations and peoples of v. 2 are more distant
antecedents. The gorged dust contrasts with YHWH's sword, in v. 6,
that is gorged with fat. The four initial waws punctuate v. 7 into four
separate statements in the Hebrew; this is an effect that cannot be easily
rendered in English.

'Go down', a *weqatal* form, repeats the action of YHWH's sword in
v. 5b and of the leaves in v. 4, while 'drinks its fill', another *weqatal*
form, seconds the sword's condition in 5a (see p. 48). Now it is the
land, the dust, that is soaked and gorged with blood and fat. The connection implies a cause and effect, a narrative, that, typical of the poet's
style, is not described explicitly; the sword descends, animals are
slaughtered and fall and the ground is drenched with their blood, but no
action or actor is listed as the explicit cause. The focus is on the victims
and their gruesome conditions.

'Land' or 'earth' (both are meanings of אֶרֶץ; see v. 1) and 'dust',

---

31. Note the particular variation in the use of the root דשׁן. In 7d a pual *yiqtol*
occurs while a hothpael *qatal* appears in v. 6b. See GKC 54h and Waltke and
O'Connor 1990: 422 and 432 for discussion of the forms.

32. For 'wild ox(en)', רְאֵמִים, see Num. 23.22 and 24.8 (a metaphor for YHWH),
Deut. 33.17 and Ps. 22.22. For 'bull', אַבִּיר, see Isa. 46.12; 1 Sam. 21.8 and Jer.
46.15. The biform אֲבִיר refers to YHWH in Isa. 1.24, 49.26 and 60.16. 'Young bull',
פַּר, is a sacrificial animal in Exod. 24.5 and 29.10-14.

עָפָר, are a frequent pair in the Hebrew Bible and in Isaiah (see Watson 1984: 357). In Isaiah they connote complete humiliation, being totally laid low. 'The high fortifications of your walls he brings down, lays low, reduces to the ground [אֶרֶץ], to the very dust [עָפָר]' (25.12). 'The lofty city he lays low; he lays it low to the ground, reduces it to dust' (26.5).

> From lower than the ground, you [Jerusalem] will speak; from beneath
> the dust, your words;
> Like a ghost from the ground, your voice; from the dust, your words you
> will chirp (29.4).[33]

In 34.7 they combine to emphasize the totality of the drenching effect of the blood and the fat with the added connotation that all has been brought low. The connotation will carry over into the scenes of vv. 9-13.

From the Heavens to the Earth. In the opening section of our poem, the poet maintains a cosmic view that is a God's-eye point of view. He surveys the effects of the divine wrath on the entire earth and on the heavens from a stance that is beyond them both. Given this viewpoint, it is then fitting that YHWH can, in a sense, interrupt the poet by speaking 'from heaven'. In his brief intervention, YHWH gives presence to and affirms the action of his sword in the heavens and its imminent descent to the earth. The sword is a familiar biblical symbol for violence, blood and death. YHWH's sword is 'cruel, large and strong' (Isa. 27.1; see 66.16). Its descent corresponds inversely to the ascent of the stench of corpses (v. 3) that imagistically moved the poet from describing earthly effects to describing heavenly effects. The descent matches the poet's shift, in the rest of the poem, to the earthly realm.

And it fits the tenor of the poem that it is YHWH's sword and not the deity himself who is active. This is a poem focused on the effects of divine wrath and comfort and not on the deity or his actions. And it is not a poem spoken by YHWH except for this short assertion (and perhaps part of 34.16). Indeed, the transition between the two main parts of the poem is the request to consult YHWH's scroll, not YHWH himself. The poet, to put it bluntly, gives short shrift to YHWH. He moves

---

33. I note but do not develop the fact that 'earth' and 'dust' can refer to death and the underworld as in 2.9-21, 14.9-12 and this passage cited from 29.4. See Tromp 1969: 85-89 for discussion and further examples, both biblical and extra-biblical.

him off center-stage to give room for the impressive scenes in the poem. This partly explains why some, for example, Wildberger (see above, p. 49), have wanted to emend the two first-person pronouns to third-person pronouns and turn even this verse into a description of YHWH.

In contrast to the poet's cosmic view, YHWH focuses on his sword and on its particular earthly target or targets: Edom (and) his doomed people. Following upon the divine utterance, the poet concentrates on the effects of the divine rage on the earth. The rolled and withered heavens are left behind for the remainder of the poem. 'Edom' and 'my doomed people' can be read as obvious synonyms; this is the rendering and understanding of most translations and commentaries. However, this translation requires one to gloss over the waw on the preposition על that introduces the phrase 'on my doomed people [on the-people-of my-ban]'.

> Lo, it will descend upon Edom,
> upon the people I have doomed to judgment (NRSV).

> Lo, it shall come down in judgment
> upon Edom, a people I have doomed (NAB).

> See, it comes down on Edom,
> on the people that he has dedicated to judgment (Wildberger 1982: 1325).

I translate the bicolon as setting a parallel between Edom and YHWH's doomed people and take the waw on 5c as emphatic. 'It comes down on Edom, yes, on my doomed people'. This rendering still leaves open the question of whether the parallel asserts the identity of 'Edom' and 'my doomed people' or whether it presents them as a pair, as two different groups that are condemned. In this vein, we can translate 'It comes down on Edom, even on my doomed people'. Although I leave the question open, I do maintain the latter alternative as an integral part of the reading. This is not a claim that this is the only way to understand the parallel, that this is the 'true interpretation'; rather, it is an emphasis on the alternative since it is seldom considered such in other commentaries.

In v. 2, YHWH's wrath and doom fall on all the nations. In v. 5, then, YHWH could focus on one or two of these nations. The most obvious candidate for 'the people of my doom' is Israel who are 'the people of my anger' in 10.6 (see above, p. 49). At another point YHWH declares that Israel was once subject to the ban.

> Your [Israel] first father sinned and your leaders rebelled against me. I disgraced the holy princes and I handed Jacob over to doom [the ban] and Israel to condemnation (43.28).

Thus, in 34.5, YHWH could be declaring that his sword descends on Edom and also on Israel, the people he has handed over to the ban.

This is the same fantastic style of reading proposed and discussed in relation to the analysis of v. 4. It is a reading that hovers between alternatives and does not finally decide for one or the other. To this point our poem is a proclamation of the grim fate of the nations, particularly that of Edom, that alludes to and contains traces of times of victory and prosperity. Through v. 4 it was possible to read the grim message as addressed to the nations and the positive traces as addressed to Israel. However, to insert Israel, either by direct reference or by allusion, into v. 5 as an object of YHWH's bloody sword blocks this possibility. The devastation befalls Israel and then there is no obvious addressee for the latent and hopeful message, and we are still hovering between alternative interpretations. I reiterate my earlier point that Isaiah's vision is not a simplistic morality tale in which ultimately Israel wins and all others lose. Israel, as all other humans and human groups, can win, lose or draw. But let us read on to see how this style of reading works itself out in this poem.

Animals: The Encyclopedic Quality. In this comparatively brief poem, the poet employs a large number of terms for both plants and animals and repeats only two of them; I discussed plant imagery previously (see above, pp. 42-43) and turn now to the animals. Animal imagery, similar to vegetal imagery, permeates the vision of Isaiah from the ox and the ass of 1.3 to the swine, vermin and mice of 66.17. The poet uses approximately 100 different terms for animals with about one-half of them occurring only once in Isaiah. He covers the gamut of beasts, fish and birds, both domestic and wild, ranging from small to large.[34]

---

34. An example of the lexical diversity occurs in 66.17. 'Swine', חזיר, occurs three times in Isaiah at the end of the book: 65.4, 66.3, 66.17. Both 'vermin', שקץ, and 'mice', עכבר, occur only in 66.17. Isaiah maintains his lexical inclusiveness until his final verse. 'Horror' or 'abhorrence' in 66.24, דראון, occurs only once more in the Hebrew Bible, in Dan. 12.2 'which is probably alluding to this passage

In our poem there are 21 terms for animals or creatures—lambs, goats and rams (34.6); wild oxen, young bulls and bulls (34.7); desert owl, screech owl, great owl and raven (34.11); jackals and ostriches (34.13); demons, phantoms, hairy beast and Lilith (34.14); owl[35] and vultures (34.15); deer[36] (35.6); and lion and ravenous beast (35.9). Of these creatures, 'desert owl', קָאַת, 'great owl', יַנְשׁוּף, 'Lilith', לִילִית, 'owl', קִפּוֹז, and 'vultures', דַּיּוֹת, each occur once in Isaiah. Lilith appears only here in the Hebrew Bible. 'Jackals' is used twice in 34.13 and 35.7 in the same contexts where 'grass' is repeated. The animals include domestic animals that are both suitable and unsuitable for sacrifice and food, normal wild animals such as the lion and the abnormal or demonic creatures of the desert.

Combined with the variety of other vocabulary and speech forms, some of which I have commented on (see above, pp. 33-35), these data testify to Isaiah's encyclopedic quality, his play with sameness and variety and his all-inclusive drive. Isaiah strives for a vision that encompasses the human world, God's word and his/its presence in the world, and he strives to present this vision in as many ways as he possibly can. These data, in addition, attest to the poet's desire to encapsulate, or at least to connect with, this wide-ranging vision in this one poem. We will continue to stop at points in the reading to assess the impact of the detail and of the great variety.

34.8-9

8   Yes, a day of vengeance for YHWH,
        a year of retribution for Zion's case.
9   Her wadis turn to pitch,[37]
        and her dust to brimstone.
    And her land is
        burning pitch.

Like the final bicolon in v. 6, v. 8 is both a conclusion to, a punctuation of, the preceding and an explanation for it. The preceding is immediately v. 7 but it then extends to vv. 2-7 through the grammatical parallel

in Isaiah. The term may have been coined by Isaiah to denote the unique disgust with the rebels' (Miscall 1993: 149).

    35. This 'owl', קִפּוֹז, differs from 'screech owl', קִפּוֹד (v. 11), only by its final letter.

    36. 'Deer', אַיָּל, is very close in spelling and sound to 'ram', אַיִל, in 34.6.

    37. I translate 'wadis', rather than the usual 'streams', to parallel the dryness denoted by 'dust'.

with YHWH's wrath and sword in vv. 2 and 5. This is the fourth and final occurrence of the phrase '*noun* + ליהוה' and the poet varies his syntax once again. This is similar to vv. 2a-b and 6e-f in that there are two initial parallel clauses and to v. 6a-b in that two *weqatal*s follow. However, here the initial noun and its parallel are construct phrases, 'day of vengeance' and 'year of retribution' and the final colon comprises a participle, בֹּעֵרָה, not a *yiqtol*.

'Day' and 'year' are the first of a group of terms for time that occur in 34.10, 17 and 35.10. As a pair they connote a long and perhaps an unlimited period of time. '[YHWH] has sent me...to proclaim a year of favor for YHWH and a day of vengeance for our God' (61.1-2; see 63.4 cited below, p. 65).

Vengeance, נקם, and retribution, שלומים, both the nouns themselves and related verbal forms,[38] contain ideas of paying back, fulfilling and carrying out, whether the context is one of punishment or reward. At this point in our poem, it is in a context of violent rebuke but, as with other aspects of the poetry, the positive connotations linger under the surface. This mix of positive and negative meanings, manifest and latent, is present in 'for Zion's case'. This is my literal and ambiguous translation of לריב ציון.[39] Is this a case against Zion? I quoted 3.13 above (p. 49): 'YHWH rises *to-argue-his-case*'; the latter phrase is לריב and would support a translation of 34.8b such as 'to argue his case against Zion'. In 41.11, 'those who strive against you [Israel]' (NRSV) are 'the men of your dispute': אנשי ריבך; this would yield something

---

38. Retribution (שלומים) is an abstract plural occurring only here in Isaiah (see Hos. 9.7; Mic. 7.3). The verb (שלם), whether qal, piel or hiphil, is used in Isaiah for fulfilling promises (19.21; 44.26, 28), repaying past fury with comfort (57.18), repaying for evil (59.18; 65.6; 66.6), and bringing mourning to a close (60.20). The verb 'to avenge' (נקם) occurs in Isaiah only in 1.24 in the niphal. The noun 'vengeance' occurs in contexts of punishment (47.3; 59.17; 63.4) and of reward, comfort (61.2).

39. Kaiser, 'for the quarrel of Zion', and NRSV, 'by Zion's cause', reflect the ambiguity. However, a note in NRSV proposes, 'by Zion's defender', which decides the ambiguity; the title is a parallel to the proper name 'YHWH' in 8a. Watts decides the case, 'to sue on Zion's behalf' as does Wildberger who reads similar to NRSV: 'welcher für Zions Recht kämpft' ('he who fights for Zion's right'). See Watts 1987: 6 and Wildberger 1982: 1327 for discussion of proposed emendations. Lust (1989: 281), in line with his view that this introduces an original and independent oracle against Judah, takes this as a reference to Zion's rebelliousness, citing 2 Sam. 22.44 and Isa. 58.4 as parallels.

such as 'for his dispute with Zion'. This is similar to 49.25: וְאֶת־יְרִיבֵךְ
אָנֹכִי אָרִיב, 'I contend with those who contend with you'.

Or is this an action on Zion's behalf? In 51.22, YHWH 'defends his
people': יָרִיב עַמּוֹ. And if it is on her behalf, is there a distinction
between Zion and her inhabitants, that is, YHWH is for Zion but against
those in her, especially sinners? 'Sinners in Zion are frightened; trembling has seized the godless' (33.14; see 4.4). This ambiguity of city
and inhabitants also inheres in the proposals to read the phrase as a
title, such as 'Zion's Defender' or 'Zion's Advocate', in parallel with
the proper name YHWH.

Further, Zion is only the fourth proper name, with YHWH, Edom and
Bozrah, to this point in the poem and it occurs without mention of
Jerusalem or Israel which are its frequent parallels in Isaiah. The lack
of the name Israel, whether the people or the land, is notable since, at
the close of v. 6, 'Bozrah' and 'the land of Edom' are paralleled. Zion
is a name at this point whose precise denotation and connotation are not
clear. Is this just the city? Is this the city personified? Is this the city as
a synecdoche for all Israel? We will return to this topic at the next
mention of Zion in 35.10 at the close of our poem.

The ambiguity surrounding the phrase לְרִיב צִיּוֹן continues in v. 9 in
'her' wadis, 'her' dust and 'her' land. Translators and commentators
generally take Edom as the antecedent of 'her' and read vv. 9-15 as a
description of the land of Edom after its destruction witnessed in vv. 2-
7. This is one possible interpretation, well evidenced in the commentaries and translations. I offer a few examples.

> 'And the streams of Edom shall be turned into pitch' (NRSV; there is a
> note on 'Edom'—'Heb. *her streams*'—that indicates the change intro-
> duced in the translation).

> 'Edom's torrents will be turned to pitch' (REB; there is no note on
> 'Edom').

> 'Its streams shall be turned to pitch' (JPS; there is an explanatory note on
> 'Its'—'I.e. Edom's').

> 'Its streams will turn into pitch' (NJB; there is no note on 'Its').[40]

On the other hand, another possible antecedent is the immediately
preceding Zion; vv. 9-15 are then a description of Zion's land, Israel.

---

40. Wildberger (1982: 1345) doesn't identify Edom in his translations or textual
notes, but he does in his commentary on vv. 9-15 that he titles 'Die totale Zer-
störung Edoms' ('Edom's total destruction').

Zion is a city that is feminine in Isaiah (and elsewhere in the Hebrew Bible) and this would explain the 'her'. In contrast, Edom, as a country, would usually be described with a masculine pronoun as are Israel and Assyria in Isaiah (see 1.2-5; 10.5-6); if the 'her' refers back to Edom it would then be by way of the capital city, Bozrah.

To return to the poem itself, I present a different division of the material in vv. 5-9 that produces a slightly altered scenario with three main panels: first is YHWH's bloody sword descending on both Edom and the doomed people; then the gory sacrifice in Bozrah and Edom; and finally the day of vengeance 'for Zion's case'. In this division, Zion is or at least contains 'my doomed people' since Edom was the subject of the second panel. Thus this division supports a distinction between Edom and the doomed people. Verses 9-15, in this scenario, describe the desolation of 'her' land leaving the antecedent of 'her' an open question. I alter the verses' format to emphasize the three parts. In addition, this is another example of how the physical presentation of the text on the page affects our understanding of that text.

A   Yes, my sword drank its fill in the heavens!
      Now it comes down on Edom, yes, on my doomed people, for judgment.
      A sword for YHWH: it is filled with blood, it is gorged with fat,
      With the blood of lambs and goats, with the fat of the innards of rams.

B   Yes, a sacrifice for YHWH in Bozrah, and a great slaughter in the land of
           Edom.
      Wild oxen go down with them, and young bulls with bulls;
      Their land drinks its fill of blood, and their dust is gorged with fat.

C   Yes, a day of vengeance for YHWH, a year of retribution for Zion's case.
      Her wadis turn to pitch, and her dust to brimstone.
      And her land is burning pitch.

The interpretation that at least one of the antecedents of 'her' is Zion is further supported by the pun in 'her wadis' (נְחָלֶיהָ) on 'heritage' (נַחֲלָה), a designation for the land Israel (Exod. 15.17; Isa. 49.8)[41] or for the people Israel as YHWH's inheritance (Deut. 4.20; Isa. 19.25; 63.17). Verses 9-15 are multivalent in the possible identifications of the land referred to by the pronoun 'her': besides Edom and Zion/Israel, there is also Babylon and Sodom and Gomorrah. I discuss the latter below and turn now to Babylon who is compared to Sodom and Gomorrah. This is Lady Babylon who is referred to with grammatically feminine forms. In

41. For the verb, 'to give as an inheritance', see Isa. 14.2; 49.8 and 57.13.

addition to the following passage, she appears in 21.9 and ch. 47. The man, the king of Babylon, is the subject of 14.4-23. This male–female distinction is analogous to that between Israel, 'he', and Zion/Jerusalem, 'she'.

> Babylon, most beautiful of kingdoms, the proud splendor of the
>   Chaldeans will be
> Like Sodom and Gomorrah overthrown by God.
> She will never be lived in and she will not be dwelt in for all times;
> No Arab will tent there and shepherds will not rest their flocks there.
> Demons will rest there and howling creatures will fill their houses;
> Ostriches will dwell there and hairy beasts will cavort there.
> Phantoms will howl in her towers and jackals in her pleasure palaces
>   (13.19-22).

This similarity or overlap of Babylon and Israel in the male–female duality and in 34.9-15 is striking. It reaches a highpoint at the close of ch. 47. The chapter opens as a denunciation of Lady Babylon who is named in vv. 1 and 5. But from v. 8 onwards, this is a condemnation of a woman who can stand for Zion just as easily as for Babylon (see below, p. 121, for the text). Both the iniquity that she is charged with and the disasters that are predicted for her apply elsewhere in Isaiah to Zion, to Israel or the women of Israel.[42]

I am not proposing Zion as the only possible antecedent of 'her'.[43] Indeed, despite this lengthy discussion, my reading is concerned first with the description itself, its scenes and its details, and only secondarily with questions of identity. I would give this topic less attention if it were not for commentaries' near obsession with the question of

42. For the identification of the subject of ch. 47 as a woman and not as a simple personification of Babylon, see Sawyer 1989: 91: '[T]here is not one detail in this chapter that refers explicitly to a city: nothing about walls or gates or sieges. It tells the story of the overpowering and humiliation of a woman. Feminine singular forms are used throughout...The personification is complete, the story autonomous and consistent'.

I note the multiple personifications of Israel in Isaiah but don't develop them since this is not relevant to our poem. 'Israel' is masculine singular and plural; 'Zion/Jerusalem', who both stands on her own and symbolizes the people, is feminine singular; there are also the plural group of women or daughters (see 3.16-4.6 and 32.9-13). The literary relationships that exist between them in the vision can be quite complicated.

43. Lust (1989: 280-83) sees vv. 8-15 as an originally independent oracle against Judah that has been combined with those against Edom (vv. 5-6) and the nations (2-3; 7).

identity. My mode of reading is in accord with my previous comments on manifest and latent meaning and on the poet's direct and vivid style. In vv. 9-15 the poet depicts 'her land' and its inhabitants in detail. The focus is on these scenes, not on the question of whether this is meant to be Edom, Israel or Babylon. She is none of them and all of them at once.

Muilenberg, in this vein, comments that the repressed references to the land that use only pronouns and adverbs add to the 'vagueness and mysteriousness of the picture' (1940: 354 [1984: 74]). I can only agree with this and add that the fact that these pronouns and adverbs usually have unspecified antecedents augments the vagueness and mysteriousness. I note this impact at relevant points.

Verse 9a is introduced by a *weqatal* that stands in an open relation to the preceding and that also reflects the richness and openness of the Hebrew verbal system. Both bicola in v. 9 open with a *weqatal* verb, emphasizing the fact of change before listing what has in fact changed. From v. 9 onwards, the poet displays the effects of what has transpired in vv. 2-8. The description in 9a-b is introduced by the niphal of 'to change', 'to turn (in)to' (הפך). This is not a simile: the wadis turn into pitch, not something like pitch. 'Wadi' or 'stream' and 'dust' parallel the wet/dry contrast, blood/fat and dust, of 7c-d. The dust soaked in fat now turns into burning pitch. This literal, direct description continues through v. 15. In addition, as typical of the poem, the phrase is passive: 'The wadis are turned to...', not, 'YHWH turned the wadis to...'

Verse 9c-d, that I scan as two short bicola, is an enjambment depicting the change of 'her land' into burning pitch, a sharp intensification of just 'pitch' in 9a. The bicolon begins with והיתה, a *weqatal* of the copulative verb היה, that 'introduces a discussion or...advances it by introducing a situation that is only more or less loosely connected with the preceding situation' (Waltke and O'Connor 1990: 538-39). The content, the scansion, the enjambment and the initial verb all combine to give the bicolon both a concluding and a punctuating emphasis that I reflect by using the introductory 'and' and by translating 'is' rather than 'becomes'.

הפך also means to overthrow or devastate, and, with brimstone (גפרית), alludes to the destruction of Sodom and Gomorrah in Genesis 19[44] that is explicitly intoned in Isa. 13.19—Babylon is to be 'like

---

44. Mathews 1995: 62-64 discusses in more detail all the biblical references to the overthrow of Sodom and Gomorrah.

Sodom and Gomorrah overthrown by God'—and implicitly in 1.7—
'like the overthrow of aliens'—where it refers to the ruin of Judah (note
the analogy established between Babylon and Israel). In our poem the
two cities, Sodom and Gomorrah, are present through allusion in the
details of the depiction, not through explicit simile. In a sense, 'her
land' is the two cities after the divine visitation, not just like them. In
Genesis the cities are connected with Lot, the ancestor of Ammon and
Moab who are listed with Edom in Isa. 11.14. Such widening patterns
of allusion undermine any attempts to limit the scene of vv. 9-15 only
to Edom.[45]

Allusive and Elusive Reading. This phrase provides another perspective
on our style of reading that, to this point, has focused on the presentation and on the details of the manifest text and then spoken of latent
meanings, of traces and hints of meanings and connotations from parallels and of hesitating, oscillating or hovering between interpretations.
The word play on 'allusive' and 'elusive' is another attempt to express
the status of these other meanings and readings that are there and yet
not there. I have already cited the poet's use of three similes in 1.8 as a
contrast to the lack of same in 34.5-15; the same passage provides a
contrast to this mode of 'elusive allusion'. 'And daughter Zion is left
like a booth in a vineyard...like a besieged city' can more easily and
more obviously be related to the narrative of Sennacherib's siege of
Jerusalem in 701 BCE as told in Isaiah 36–37 and 2 Kgs 18.13–19.37
than 'her land is burning pitch' can be related to any particular event as
narrated in Isaiah or elsewhere in the Hebrew Bible.[46]

---

45. Seitz (1993: 237), focusing on the animals listed in vv. 6-15, speculates that
this depicts 'a scene like that prior to Noah's entering the ark (Gen. 6:19–7:3)—or
better, like that after the flood when all had been destroyed and only Noah and his
animal collection remained. This might explain the threefold reference to the
animal and his or her mate (34:14, 15, 16), as in the case of Noah, "two of every
kind...male and female" (Gen. 6:19-20)'. This accords both with my following
suggestion that the scene depicts a perverse remnant and with the clear inclusion of
both males and females in the wasted land.
  46. I recognize that I am working with a general and somewhat vague distinction to make my point concerning the style of our poem; therefore I use the impre-
cise adverbial phrases 'more easily' and 'more obviously'. I am not going to
develop the distinction or apply it elsewhere in the poem. I note that many commentators debate whether 1.8 refers to an Assyrian invasion of 734 BCE or 701 BCE.

Even with this understanding of daughter Zion in 1.8, I am working with a notion of allusion and intertextual reference. 'Daughter Zion is left...like a besieged city' is related to textual accounts of Sennacherib's siege and not to the historical event itself 'wie es eigentlich gewesen ist'.[47] The intertexts embrace Sennacherib's account of the siege that includes his own simile for Hezekiah.

> As to Hezekiah, the Jew, he did not submit to my yoke, I laid siege to 46 of his strong cities...Himself I made a prisoner in Jerusalem, his royal residence, *like a bird in a cage.* I surrounded him with earthwork in order to molest those who were leaving his citys gate (*ANET*: 288; my emphasis).

This is quite different from the approach in most commentaries on Isaiah that deal with 1.8 and the poem in 34–35 as though they were referring directly to historical events and sites of the eighth to fifth centuries BCE. To develop this contrast I need first to renew the discussion of YHWH's role in the poem, particularly any stated motivation for his wrath. The following deals both with specific readings of 34.8 in its context and with the modes of reading that underlie my and the commentaries' interpretations.

Is Judgment Justice? In his vision, Isaiah displays different relationships that exist between YHWH and humanity and between YHWH and the divisions of humanity, particularly Israel and the nations. YHWH is creator, helper, parent and savior of all, especially of Israel. At the same time, he is judge, punisher and executioner, especially of all who are violent, rebellious, wicked and arrogant. He can be in these varied roles with anyone from an individual to a whole nation. YHWH humiliates the proud whether they are Shebna (22.15-19), the king of Babylon (14.4-21) or all humanity (2.9-22). On the other hand, he supports the

---

See p. 45 n. 17 in which I discuss 1.8. My point, however, is textual, not historical. The image of isolated Zion and Jerusalem accords with the narrative in chs. 36–37; there is no similar matching narrative for the Syro-Ephraimite War.

47. This is Leopold von Ranke's oft-cited phrase, 'as it really happened', from his *Histories of the Latin and Germanic Nations from 1495 to 1514* published in 1824 (trans. P.A. Ashworth; London: Macmillan, 1887). See White 1973: 163-90 for particulars and a full discussion of von Ranke's historical work. White's work in *Metahistory* and in his other essays has been instrumental in the development of my thought on history and historiography; earlier I discussed his comments on the textual nature of historiography and historical evidence (see pp. 12-13).

righteous whether they are 'a righteous nation that maintains faith' (26.2), Hezekiah (ch. 38), his servants (65.8-16) or any human (56.1-7). The contrast is expressed in 3.10-11.

> Tell the righteous that it is good for they will eat the fruit of their work.
> Woe to the wicked! Evil will be repaid to them for what their hands have done.

In sharp contrast to this sense of justice, YHWH can choose or call someone, nation or individual, simply because he wants to regardless of their moral worth or status. His election of Israel permeates the entire book of Isaiah. As another example, he calls and supports Cyrus, his shepherd and his anointed, even though Cyrus doesn't know him (44.28–45.5). To put it in simple terms, YHWH can play favorites. Immediately after describing his subjection of Jacob to doom, the ban, YHWH proclaims his favor for him.

> Your [Israel] first father sinned and your leaders rebelled against me.
> I disgraced the holy princes and I handed Jacob over to doom and Israel
>   to condemnation.
> And now hear, O Jacob, My Servant; O Israel, whom I have chosen!
> Thus says YHWH who makes you, who fashions you in the womb—he
>   will help you:
> Do not fear, O my Servant, O Jacob! O Jeshurun, whom I have chosen!
>   (43.27–44.2).

If YHWH can step outside justice to choose a people as his own, does he also move beyond justice at the other extreme to destroy innocent people in unbridled wrath? To put it more harshly, are divine mercy and love matched by divine rage and horror? Am I justified in paralleling and juxtaposing, and not placing in a chronological sequence, the dream and fantasy of the last part of the poem with the nightmare and destruction of the first? These are the types of questions that Isaiah wrestles with and entertains a positive answer to in passages that depict YHWH's rage wreaking havoc on the world and humanity, passages such as 13.2-16, 24.1-23, 30.27-28, 54.7-8, 59.15b-19 and 63.1-6. I cite the last passage because it shares much with our poem, for example, Edom and Bozrah, wrath, blood, vengeance and redemption, and because it presents this portrait of the bloody warrior god 'trampling out the vintage where the grapes of wrath are stored'[48] without any concern to explain or justify the violence.

48. This is the opening line and scene of the American 'Battle Hymn of the Republic', the war anthem of the North in the American Civil War.

Who is this coming from Edom, in crimsoned garments, from Bozrah?
This one, splendidly attired, striding in his great might?
It is I, speaking victoriously, great to give victory!
Why is your attire red and your clothes like those of one who treads the winepress?
I've trodden the winevat alone, and there was not one from the peoples with me.
I trod on them in my anger and trampled them in my rage.
Their juice spattered on my clothes and all my robes are stained.
Yes! A day of vengeance is in my mind and the year for me to redeem has come.
I looked but there was no helper; I stared but there was no one to aid,
So my own arm brought me victory and my rage aided me.
I trampled peoples in my anger; I made them drunk with my rage; I poured out their lifeblood [juice] on the ground.

In large part, I was originally drawn to this consideration of the grim side of 'mercy'—by mercy I refer to acts that are outside a system of justice, acts that are, in effect, unjust whether they are for weal or for woe—by reading Isaiah 34–35 and some of the commentaries on it. Commentators have little or no trouble discussing YHWH's saving and restorative mercy in ch. 35, including his choice of Israel and Zion. However, with ch. 34, considerable pains are taken to justify YHWH's wrath and his horrific treatment of the nations. This imbalance led to my reading ch. 34 more closely with the suspicion that this critical concern was perhaps a reaction to a text that depicts divine rage and its aftermath without particular interest in justifying that rage.

I digress into a few of the commentaries but, since my goal is to return as soon as possible to the reading of our poem, this is not meant to be a thorough or exhaustive presentation of what commentators say on the subject. These examples are representative both of a particular justification of the divine rage and of the mode of analysis that underlies the justification. This mode, that seeks to establish clarity and the one interpretation, has, in a variety of ways, led me to develop my sharply contrasting way of reading. I begin with McKenzie's Anchor Bible commentary since it is an older work, published in 1968, and since it is one that I would have at first been very receptive to. In regard to ch. 35, he comments that

> salvation as envisaged here is for Israel alone; no attention is given to
> the nations. This narrowness is not without its compensation in some

other passages [in Isaiah 40–66]... In this area Israel's understanding of
the scope of Yahweh's saving will was still developing (1968: 12).

Later I will comment on this summary of the 'message' of ch. 35 and I
note, in passing, the ease with which McKenzie moves from a view
expressed in one chapter in the book of Isaiah to 'Israel's
understanding'.

McKenzie regards the restriction of salvation to only Israel as nar-
rowing the scope of divine salvation but it is a narrowness that will dis-
appear with time. He says nothing more about why YHWH, in the first
place, would will to save Israel or any other nation or about what he is
saving them from. But McKenzie is not so reticent about the violence
and harshness of ch. 34. He has a note on v. 8.

> *vengeance and retribution.* legal terms designating the punishment of
> one who does damages and where possible, the recovery of the damages.
> 'Vindication' and 'compensation' would correspond to the idea. But in
> Hebrew there are no distinct words for these ideas such as we have in
> English... The lack of refinement of language gives such passages as this
> a harsh tone to modern readers (1968: 5).

Is McKenzie suggesting that 63.1-6 would be less harsh if instead of
'day of vengeance' we employed a more refined phrase such as 'day of
compensation?'[49]

Wildberger (1982: 1344), followed closely by Watts (1987: 12),
argues in a similar vein. In v. 8, he translates 'Tag der Rache' ('day of
vengeance') and comments that 'Rache' is only a weak translation ('ein
Notbehelf'), since נקם is originally a legal term that refers to re-estab-
lishing the social order that has been upset by a crime. This is
confirmed by שלומים ('Vergeltung': repayment, recompense) that refers
to securing the integrity of society and its members. Wildberger then
takes the violent context into account and attempts to counter it.

> Naturally the two concepts [Rache; Vergeltung] contain a time of pun-
> ishment. The divine sentence of punishment [Strafgerechtigkeit] is
> inexorable, but it is not an end in itself; rather it is a means to an end,
> ultimately even a way to salvation [Heil].

---

49. Seitz (1993: 236-42) reveals a similar imbalance in his respective treatments
of ch. 34, which receives a little over two pages dealing mainly with the role of
Edom, and of ch. 35, which receives a short paragraph. Over half of his discussion
of the two chapters is devoted not to their content, but to the question of their relation to the rest of Isaiah, mainly Isa. 40–66.

In terms of the opening of our poem in 34.1-8, I already noted Wild-berger's explanation for the lack of a stated motivation for YHWH's wrath. He must be justified but for the poet 'the weight of guilt is so heavy that he would consider it superfluous to say anything about it' (1982: 1341; see pp. 39-40 n. 11). Watts locates the justification in the 'for judgment' in v. 5:

> *For judgment* is the equivalent of 'for good cause' or 'for reasons of justice'. The ban and Yahweh's fury through the sword have not been applied arbitrarily. The Vision assumes that its audience/readers would need no explanation of Edom's sins (1987: 10; Watts' emphasis).

McKenzie mirrors this and generalizes it.

> If Israel itself had experienced the destroying judgment of Yahweh for its rebellion, the peoples which had never accepted his sovereignty at all could hardly expect better treatment... [T]he events of the fall of Judah and the Exile acquainted the Israelites with great nations which blas-phemed the name of Yahweh in the sense that they did not confess... the lordship of Yahweh. Yahweh would have to prove his lordship by judgment (1968: 7).

Scott explains that the awe inspiring and terrible picture of ch. 34 derives from

> the conviction that the righteous will of Yahweh must ultimately prevail on the earth. The clash between good and evil, between the Creator, the Lord of history, and the forces which defy him, must be resolved in the end (1956: 354).

Such a powerful need to justify, if not to explain away, divine wrath and destruction for me testified, and still testifies, to a deep unease with the violence and gore of an Isaianic passage such as 34.1-15 and 63.1-6. If YHWH can be merciful and compassionate without moral motiva-tion, can't he also be brutal and wrathful without moral motivation? (I note that Job would answer this with a resounding Yes!) Let me con-tinue the discussion and the reading to explore this question and to assess the impact of the violent and grotesque scenes of the poem.

I began this lengthy analysis of possible motives for the divine rage as a way to further the exploration of the commentaries that consis-tently seek to understand our poem, and its parts, as referring, directly or indirectly, to historical events or periods.[50] It is maintained that

---

50. In his final comment on ch. 34, McKenzie generalizes this historical expla-nation in what, to me, is another attempt to distance the violence and its aftermath

God's wrath is a legitimate response to the evil of the nations in general and of Edom in particular whether this refers to a specific act of Edom at the time of the fall of Jerusalem or to the general hostility between Edom and Judah (see Mathews 1995: 69-119; Wildberger 1982: 1335-41, 1344-45).

Yet in the poem itself, and in some of the other depictions of divine rage as in 63.1-6, little, if anything, is said about any reasons for the rage. Even if we take the terms 'judgment' or 'justice', 'vengeance' and 'retribution' in the positive and refined senses advocated by the commentators, we still have to supply, as they do, initial crimes or sins that are being judged and justly repaid. What have the nations, Edom, Israel or anyone done that is so terrible that it could justify this violent and gruesome reaction or that in 63.1-6? (Job still lingers in the background, nodding his head in agreement.)

Further, I think that this need to justify YHWH and to justify him conclusively explains, in part, the strong consensus that vv. 9-15 describe the desolation of Edom. A solid justification or motivation for violent judgment requires a clearly defined criminal, that is, Edom, who must be guilty of a sufficiently horrendous crime or crimes.[51] The latter are not listed but the poem's 'audience/readers would need no explanation of Edom's sins' (Watts 1987: 10; see McKenzie 1968: 7). But our reading of the poem to this point reveals no such clarity or decisiveness either about the object of YHWH's wrath and vengeance (other than the general category of the nations and their armies) or about why he is against them. There is detail and precision on the fury, the violence and their aftermath, but there is no mention of any of the usual motivations

---

from YHWH. The grim details mirror both reality and popular demonology: 'Even in the exilic period the number of abandoned sites in the ancient Near East was large enough to permit biblical writers to portray such sites with convincing realism; Jerusalem itself was one after the catastrophe of 587 BC. Such sites were abandoned by the gods, whose cult was no longer carried on there, and they became haunts of demons. This popular demonology is reflected both in this passage and in Isa. xiii, on which this passage depends. The existence of such abandoned cities, we may be sure, gave a certain force to the biblical proclamations of God's judgments' (1968: 8).

51. Even though Lust (1989: 280-83) regards vv. 8-15 as an original and independent oracle against Judah, not Edom, this only results in Judah becoming the guilty culprit. Lust is not pursuing the mode of plural reading employed in this study.

of sin, rebellion, pride or iniquity. The opening of Isaiah's vision stands
in sharp contrast to our poem.

> Children I rear and bring up, but they rebel against me.
> The ox knows its owner, and the donkey the crib of its master;
> Israel does not know, my people do not understand.
> Woe! Sinful nation; iniquitous people;
> offspring of evil-doers; children who act corruptly!
> They have forsaken YHWH; they have despised the Holy One of Israel;
> they have turned back (1.2-4).

Instead of producing an obvious object and motive for the rage, the
poem has been a study in the production of multiple readings and in
ferreting out the traces of other readings whether they are called 'latent
meanings', 'shadow readings' or 'elusive allusions'. We will have
opportunity to comment further on this emphasis on justifying YHWH's
violence in our treatment of the beginning of the second part of the
poem.

34.10

10　Night and day it does not extinguish;
　　　　forever her smoke goes up;
　　　　from generation to generation she is desolate;
　　　　for an eternity of eternities none pass through her.

'Night and day' is the second temporal phrase in the poem, after 'day'
and 'year' in v. 8, and the first of four in this quatrain. This is another
excellent example of Isaiah's play with regularity—that is, the theme of
time—and variety—that is, four different phrases in one quatrain. All
four phrases combine to denote an everlasting, unending state. As in the
rest of the poem, I translate the quatrain with a present tense, rather
than the usual future, to capture this unending quality that we see in an
eternal now.

In addition, the phrase 'night and day' alludes to the day and night,
the evening and morning, of Genesis 1, an allusion made more explicit
by the poet's trope on תהו ובהו in v. 11.[52] The multivalent scene of
devastation that follows in vv. 10-15 is, then, a perverted or demonic
creation, yet just to posit the term creation is to keep the creation of
Genesis hovering under the surface of our poem.

---

52. See Miscall 1992: 49-50 for analysis of the parallels between Isaiah and
Genesis.

'Not to extinguish' or 'not to be quenched', כבה, alludes to the unquenchable fires at the close of chs. 1 and 66; the image occurs at the beginning, middle and end of Isaiah and this underscores the fact that our poem is in the center of the book.

> They burn, the two of them together,
> And there is no one to quench them (1.31).

> They go out and see the bodies of the people who rebel against me.
> Their worm never dies; their fire is never to be quenched; and finally,
> they are a horror to all flesh (66.24).[53]

YHWH's servant 'will not quench a dimly burning wick' (42.3), but the powerful lie down and 'are quenched like a wick' (43.17). In the overall vision, the poet uses the concept and image of (not) quenching with opposing connotations; this accords with our emphasis on Isaiah's encyclopedic quality and with the reading of this part of the poem as a manifest nightmare covering a latent dream. It is also another example of how one image can help to bind the entire vision together.

The quatrain has a complicated poetic structure. Cola 10a and d are negative while 10b and c are positive; this encloses the quatrain in a chiasmus of negative : positive :: positive : negative. The three *yiqtol* verbs in 10a, b and c are followed by a participle at the end of 10d that rounds off the quatrain. (Note the parallel with the participle at the close of v. 9.) The use of *yiqtol* verbs and the participle, rather than *weqatal* as in v. 9, allows each colon to open with and to stress the temporal phrase. As noted previously, the poet varies his use of verb forms for the poetic effects of structure and variation just as much as for syntactical and grammatical rules (see above, p. 39). Finally, in the quatrain the poet continues to develop his overall panorama by means of individual scenes.

Rising smoke echoes both the rising stench of v. 3 and the descending sword of v. 5; it looks back to the fire image of 9.17-18 that I cited previously on p. 30 n. 2.

> Wickedness indeed burns like fire; it consumes briers and thorns;
> It kindles the thickets of the forest; they billow up in a column of smoke.

In Isaiah, characteristic of his multivalent use of imagery, smoke connotes the guiding column of the Exodus (4.5), the divine presence in the temple (6.1-5), the transience of material creation (51.6) and vexation, 'smoke in my [YHWH's] nose' (65.5).

---

53. See below, pp. 135-36, for comments on the translation.

From 34.9 through 35.10, I consistently translate Hebrew feminine pronouns with 'she' and 'her', even though the antecedent or reference may not be clear or univocal. This translation maintains the vague and mysterious atmosphere of the depiction. In addition, it continues the possibility that the description is of the land belonging to a city whether that city be Bozrah, Zion or even Babylon, but to continue it as the latent or allusive meaning and not as a firm identification that cancels the vague atmosphere. This issue of the feminine pronouns and their ambiguous antecedents is glossed over in most translations that render them with 'it' or 'its'.

> Night and day it shall never go out;
> Its smoke shall rise for all time.
> Through the ages it shall lie in ruins;
> Through the aeons none shall traverse it (JPS).

Word- and Root-Play. 'To be desolate', 'to be dry' or 'to be a waste', חרב, puns on the sword (חֶרֶב) in vv. 5-6; this forms a trio of similar roots and terms: חרם (to doom: vv. 2 and 5), חֶרֶב and חרב. In biblical Hebrew, the root חרב occurs as a verb and in two nominal forms, חֹרֶב and חָרְבָּה, in a variety of contexts with different connotations. I cite some examples because they are relevant to this context and to that in the latter part of the poem (35.1-7); I limit myself to passages that employ this root. First, the root can denote the ruins, devastation or des- iccation which are the result of divine punishment. Indeed, the power to dry up the wet is evidence of divine might. In the following passage, note that YHWH darkens the heavens (see 13.10), an image that is anal- ogous to their rolling up in 34.4 (see above, p. 40).

> Is my hand too short to redeem; don't I have the power to deliver?
> By my mere shout I *dry up* sea, I turn rivers into wilderness;
> Their fish stink from lack of water, they lie dead from thirst.
> I clothe the heavens with blackness and cover them with sackcloth (50.2-
> 3; see 44.27).[54]

The first of the following three citations refers to the destruction of both Israel and humanity and includes animal imagery.

> And the lambs graze as in their pasture, and among *the ruins* fatlings and
> aliens feed (5.17).

54. The passage contains the motif of stench and the same root באש that occur in 34.3: 'Their corpses: their stench [בָּאְשָׁם] goes up' (see above, p. 32).

> Waters disappear from the sea; the Nile is *parched* and dry.
> Canals stink; the branches of Egypt's Nile are totally *parched*; reed and
> rush rot (19.5-6).

> Your holy cities have become a wilderness; Zion has become a
> wilderness; Jerusalem is desolate.
> Our holy and beautiful house, where our fathers praised you,
> Has been burned with fire, and all our pleasant sites have become a *ruin*
> (64.9-10).

On the other hand, YHWH proclaims that the ruins are to be restored
and rebuilt as a sign of his salvific power. 'Your builders move faster
than your destroyers and *those who ruined you* leave you...your *ruins*
and your wastes and your destroyed land' are to be restored (49.17-19).

> They rebuild the ancient *ruins* [חָרְבוֹת]; the old desolate sites they erect;
> They re-establish the *ruined* [חֳרֶב] cities, the desolate sites of long ago
> (61.4).[55]

In summary, citing passages that include this one root produces a
group of parallels to our poem, parallels that describe the devastation of
the world, of Israel and of Egypt and that also depict the reversal of that
destruction. The group could be greatly expanded if, in addition, we
examined the other roots and words that refer to ruins, desolate sites
and devastated cities and countries, but this would take us far beyond
the scope of this study. Just as all the other Isaianic passages that I cite,
these demonstrate that the poem and its images are an integral part of
the entire book of Isaiah. Finally, from the point of view of the reading
that we are pursuing, I quote such parallel passages from within Isaiah
to enrich and enlarge the reading and appreciation of the poem, even if
this enrichment means more possible interpretations and an increase in
'elusive allusions'. I am not trying to prove some point about the relative dates of passages or so-called redactional levels within Isaiah, nor
am I using the passages to demonstrate that 34.9-15 are describing a
particular land, whether Israel or another nation.

The last colon, in its final phrase 'none pass through her', emphasizes
that the land is untraversable, not just that no one is in her. Watts's rendering makes this clear: 'No one will be passing through it' (note the
neuter 'it'). A similar image with the same word, עָבֵר, occurs in 33.8,
with no specific area described, and in 60.15, which is addressed to

---

55. 'Ancient' is the same word as 'forever' in 34.10b, עוֹלָם, and 'long ago',
דוֹר וָדוֹר, is very close to 'from generation to generation', מִדּוֹר לְדוֹר, in 34.10c.

Zion, and these parallels keep open the range of possible references of 'her' at the close of 34.10.

> Highways are deserted; *those who pass by* on the road have ceased.
> A covenant is broken; cities rejected; humanity disregarded (33.8).

> Instead of being forsaken and hated and with *none passing through*,
> I make you an object of pride forever, a joy for all generations (60.15).

In the next passage, not being able to pass through marks Zion as impenetrable, invulnerable to attack by sea. With the restoration promised in 60.15, this scene provides a faint hint of a positive note in the gloomy picture of ch. 34.

> Envision Zion, our festive city! Your eyes see Jerusalem…
> Indeed majestic YHWH will be there for us: a place of broad rivers and streams
> Where no ship with oars can go and no stately ship *pass through* (33.20-21).

'Passing through her' (עֹבֵר בָּהּ) rhymes with בֹּעֵרָה in 9d and עֲפָרָהּ in 9b; this literally connects 'none passing through her' with burning pitch and dust that is brimstone. The first two words of the set of three employ the same consonants, ב, ר and ע, although in different order. Watson (1984: 239-41) refers to this poetic device as root play; it gives a cohesion to the poem on both phonetic and semantic levels. I could readily expand the examples by including roots with only two of the consonants or with consonants that are similar in sound, for example, the voiced labial פ in עפר, but limit myself to these three consonants.[56] I first commented on the root play in a note on v. 2 in regard to the absence of עברב, 'anger', there and elsewhere in the poem despite its comprising the three consonants (see above, p. 30 n. 2). The root play continues in 'raven', עֹרֵב, in v. 11b and in 'desert', עֲרָבָה, in 35.1b.

34.11-13b

11 But they possess her, the desert owl and the screech owl,
       and the great owl[57] and the raven dwell in her;

---

56. The series could be expanded by including the root play with חרב, 'sword' and 'dry', since it shares two consonants, ב and ר, and ע and ח are both gutturals.

57. I follow NIV and Watts in this translation of three types of owl. Identification of the birds or animals is conjectural. For example, NRSV renders these three 'hawk', 'hedgehog' and 'owl' and adds a note 'Identification uncertain'. I match these three types of owl with just 'owl' in v. 15.

He stretches over her the line of desolation,
> and the weights of nothingness [next to][58] her nobles;
12   There is Not There a Kingdom they name [her],
> and all her princes are Nothing.
13   For thorns go up over her fortresses;[59]
> nettles and brambles in her strongholds.

In the first bicolon, 11a-b, the poet shifts from large animals to smaller animals, particularly birds, unacceptable for either sacrifice or food. The list is punctuated with four waws. The bicolon opens with a *weqatal* verb that is linked with the preceding and that, at the same time, marks a shift to a new scene. Despite the unceasing fire, animals do dwell in her. The bicolon, in v. 11b, closes with a *yiqtol*. This same structure, in which a bicolon begins with a *weqatal* and ends with a *yiqtol* verb, occurs in vv. 4b-c and 7c-d. With the change of verb forms, the poet is able to construct the bicolon in an envelope structure with the verbs of living framing the group of four animals that, as a group, can be taken as the subject of both verbs.[60]

58. The text is difficult if not corrupt at this point. 'Her nobles' may represent a misplaced variant of 'her princes' in the next bicolon; this conjecture underlies JPS that moves the phrase to v. 12: 'It shall be called, "No kingdom is there", its nobles and all its lords shall be nothing'. NJB connects the phrase with v. 12 but makes it the subject of the verb 'to call, name': 'There will be no more nobles to proclaim the royal authority'. A word or words may have been omitted by a scribe. Watts (1987: 4-6) translates '(What has become of) its nobles?' Wildberger (1982: 1328) employs an ellipsis and brackets: 'die Steine der Leere ... [12] [seine Edlen]'. He maintains that a verb matching 'the stones of nothingness' is expected in the place of 'its nobles' to parallel 11c, but he does not suggest a possible replacement. Unlike JPS and NJB, he thinks that the phrase makes no sense as the beginning of v. 12.

My reading follows MT with '[next to]' supplied to make sense of the text, but this is conjectural and is not meant to negate the preceding proposals and discussions. In this reading, I visualize the plumbline set next to the nobles (Amos 7.7-9). This is similar to NRSV—'and the plummet of chaos over its nobles'—and its text note: 'Heb lacks *over*'. Because of the textual uncertainty, I begin v. 12 with 'There is Not ... ' which I mark as 12a.

59. The Hebrew has an unusual syntax. I take 'fortresses' as a singular with the third person feminine singular verb and 'thorns' as an accusative phrase without a preposition; see GKC 117z and the parallel in Isa. 5.6. 'It shall come up [it shall be overgrown] with briers and thorns'. 'Land' can also be understood to be the subject: 'she will go up, as to her fortresses, with thorns'.

60. The framing effect is increased by the assonance of the verb forms: וִירֵשׁוּהָ (*vîrēšûhā*) and יִשְׁכְּנוּ־בָהּ (*yiškᵉnû-bā*).

To possess (ירשׁ) often denotes Israel's possession of the land including both its conquest and its division (Deut. 1.8; Josh. 1.11).

> I bring forth descendants from Jacob and from Judah heirs [√ירשׁ] for my
> mountains.
> My chosen inherit [ירשׁ] the land, and my servants dwell [שׁכן] there (Isa.
> 65.9).

'To dwell', שׁכן, denotes both human (Gen. 14.13; Isa. 65.9) and
divine habitation (Exod. 24.16; Deut. 12.5). 'YHWH of Hosts who
dwells on Mount Zion' (Isa. 8.18; see 57.15). In Isa. 13.20-21, the
description of the desolation of Lady Babylon, the verb refers to wastes
in which humans don't dwell but ostriches do (34.13d).

> She will never be lived in and she will not be *dwelt in* for all times...
> Ostriches *will dwell* there and hairy beasts will cavort there.[61]

'He stretches', the first word in the second bicolon, 11c-d, is a
weqatal form that, with 'they possess', frames the *yiqtol*, 'they dwell';
because of the textual problems, we cannot be certain of the close of the
bicolon (see p. 74 n. 58). In a sense the stretching, the measuring, is the
cause of the dwelling and the possession and is an echo of Joshua's
division of the land that led to Israel's possession of his land. The
phrase can be translated with the English perfect tense, 'he has
stretched over her', that supports this narrative sense of the phrase.
There is no clear antecedent for the subject 'he'. It is often assumed that
YHWH is the subject, but he is not otherwise present in this part of the
poem. Wildberger (1982: 1325, 1328) translates impersonally, 'man
spannt' ('one stretches'). The same impersonal usage can be found in v.
12a in the phrase 'they name or call [her]' as in JPS: 'It shall be called'.

Stretching out 'the line', קו, and 'the weights' (literally 'the stones'),
אבנים, is an image of the destruction of Jerusalem in the condemnation
of King Manasseh. 'I stretch out over Jerusalem the line of Samaria and
the plummet [משׁקלת] of King Ahab; I wipe Jerusalem clean as one
wipes a dish clean, wiping it and turning it' (2 Kgs 21.13). Only the
first part of the image occurs in the following scene from Lamentations.

> YHWH determined to smash the wall of daughter Zion;
> He stretched out the line, he didn't restrain his hand from destroying
> (Lam. 2.8).

---

61. The passage 13.19-22 is cited above, p. 60, in the discussion of the dual
male and female identity of Babylon and Israel.

However, this is a positive image of restoration in Zech. 1.16 since the line measures and lays out an area for construction (see Ezek. 47.3).

> Therefore thus says YHWH, 'I have returned to Jerusalem in compassion; my house will be built in her'—saying of YHWH of hosts—'and a line will be stretched over Jerusalem'.

As with so many aspects of the poem in Isaiah 34–35, we encounter multiple and contrasting meanings for this one image. Both the positive and negative connotations are contained in Isa. 28.14-19, a denunciation of Jerusalem's rulers who have entered into a covenant with Death, an agreement with Sheol, that they think will shield them from destruction. God's response includes the enigmatic statement about a solid stone in Zion; this accords with the building image of the line and plummet and literally connects with 'the stones' of 34.11. It is an image with heavily negative implications for the deluded rulers of Jerusalem but with positive implications for Zion and for those in her who trust in YHWH.

> Therefore thus says lord YHWH:
> 'See, I am laying in Zion a stone [אֶבֶן],
> A massive stone, a fine cornerstone for a foundation,
> An unshakeable foundation for one who trusts.[62]
> I make justice the measuring line [קָו] and righteousness the plummet [מִשְׁקֹלֶת].
> Hail sweeps away the false refuge and waters flood your shelter' (28.16-17).

The positive value of the image of stretching out the line accords with the divine creator's ability to stretch out the heavens (see above, p. 40). 'He creates the heavens and stretches them out' (42.5; see 44.24; 45.12; 51.13). In Job 38 the image refers to the creation of the earth and it includes the specific mention of the line. 'And who stretched a line over her [the earth]?' (v. 5). This value contrasts with YHWH's powerful outstretched hand that describes his destructive power.

> Therefore the anger of YHWH was kindled against his people, and he stretched out his hand against them and he struck them...
> For all this his anger has not turned away, and his hand is stretched out still (5.25).[63]

---

62. See Roberts 1987: 27-37 for discussion of the text of 28.16 and for an explanation of this translation that is virtually the same as his.
63. See 9.11, 16, 21; 10.4 and 14.26-27.

This image, then, refers to divine power both to create and to destroy. Creation, indeed the pre-creation state of chaos, is alluded to in 'desolation' and 'nothingness' (תהו and בהו) that are combined in the 'formless void' (NRSV), תהו ובהו, of Gen. 1.2. 'The line of desolation' and 'the weights of nothingness' may be understood as carpenter's tools that either cause the formless void of this land—'the chaotic line' and 'the voiding weights'—or are specifically meant to measure what is already a formless void—'the line for chaos' and 'the weights for the void'.

'The city of chaos' (קרית תהו) is the symbol of evil power that must be brought down (24.10), and YHWH regards parts of his creation, mainly nations, their rulers and the idolmakers, as nothing (תהו: 40.17, 23; 41.29; 44.9). In another passage, he asserts that his creation is not meaningless.

> Thus says YHWH, creator of the heavens... fashioner of the earth and its maker.
> *Not chaos* did he create it, for habitation did he fashion it.
> 'I am YHWH... I do not speak in secret, in a hiding place in a dark land;
> I do not say to Jacob's descendants, "Seek me in *chaos*" ' (45.18-19).[64]

Chaos and creation are a powerful combination of opposites that are contained by both direct statement and by allusion in our poem, particularly in the words and images of v. 11c-d. The manifest demonic creation covers over a latent divine and beneficent creation.

34.12 is susceptible of different translations and interpretations. Watts's rendering is distinct:

> Nothing there can be called a kingdom.
> All her princes are wiped out.

This is echoed in NIV:

> Her nobles will have nothing there to be called a kingdom,
> all her princes will vanish away.[65]

REB offers yet another possibility:

> No king will be acclaimed there,
> and all its princes will come to naught.

---

64. See Miscall 1992: 49-50 for further discussion of the passages and their relation to Gen. 1.

65. On p. 74 n. 58 I discuss the textual problems of v. 12 and suggested solutions.

My translation reflects the frequency of naming in Isaiah and accords
with JPS: 'It shall be called, "No kingdom is there" '. (I indicate the
status as name with capitalization and not quotation marks.) The two
titles are proper names of a sort, but they are not the same as names
such as YHWH and Zion since their reference, 'she', is not identifiable.
Following are other examples of naming in Isaiah that further display
our poem's place in the book. After the refining that YHWH conducts,
Jerusalem is called (קרא) 'The City of Righteousness, The Capital
Faithful' (1.26) and she is renamed again later in the book.

> You will no longer be called Forsaken
> And your land will no longer be called Desolation
> But you will be named [קרא] My Delight is in Her and your land
>   Married
> For YHWH delights in you and your land is married (62.4).[66]

Lady Babylon's destruction is announced with a similar notice of the
loss of a previous name but without any announcement of a new name.
The title, 'Mistress of Kingdoms', is reminiscent of 34.12, 'Not There a
Kingdom'.

> Come, sit in the dust, maiden daughter Babylon!
> Sit on the ground dethroned, daughter Chaldea!
> For they will *never again call you* Tender or Delicate...
> Sit in silence; go into darkness, daughter Chaldea!
> For they will *never again call you* Mistress of Kingdoms (47.1, 5).

In addition, I note the several meanings of קרא in Isaiah that come
into play in our poem: to call, cry out and proclaim (6.3-4; 12.4); to
name (7.14; 8.3); to read (29.11-12; 34.16)[67] and to meet and befall
(7.3; 41.2). Reading is an integral part of the poem through the references to a scroll in vv. 4 and 16 and through the explicit command to
read the scroll in v. 16.

'They name/call' in 12a, יקראו, can be taken as an impersonal or
passive construction as in Watts and JPS; there is then no need to identify the subject of the verb. 'Nothing there *can be called* a kingdom'
(Watts 1987: 4). If the verb is taken as active, then the subject 'they'

66. Naming or renaming are a frequent motif in Isaiah and occur throughout the
book; other examples are in 4.3, 7.14, 8.3, 9.5, 19.18, 45.3, 56.7, 58.12, 60.14 and
65.15.

67. Conrad (1991: 137, 143) maintains that 'to read' is one meaning of the verb
in 40.6. 'A voice says, "Read!" and I said, "What shall I read?"' This makes 40.6 a
direct reference to the proclamation that the deaf will hear or read a scroll in 29.18.

can be a reference to the nations summoned in v. 1 who then name or title the land or 'they' can be a reference to the inhabitants of the land who thereby name their own land. A final twist on the bicolon and on the verb קרא, in anticipation of v. 16, would have one of these latter groups reading about the place and its name in YHWH's scroll.

Verse 12 is enclosed by the two negative particles 'there is not', אין,[68] and 'nothing', אֶפֶס, emphasizing the void, the nullity, already intoned in the תהו and בהו of the preceding bicolon. In 5.8 אפס occurs in a setting similar to that of אין in v. 12: 'until *there is no* place left'.[69] אפס occurs with both אין and תהו in 40.17.

> All the nations are like nullity [אין] to him;
> Like nothing [אפס] and chaos [תהו] are they regarded by him.

Absolute nullity is denoted by the hendiadys 'like nullity and like nothingness [כאין וכאפס]' in 41.12. The latter pair of terms also denote divine uniqueness. '*There is not another* [אפס] besides me; I am YHWH and *there is no* [אין] other' (45.6; see 45.14 and 46.9). Or at least the claim to such. Lady Babylon says in her heart, 'I am and there is none other but me [אפסי עוד]' (47.8, 10).

Thus the two bicola in vv. 11c-12b accentuate the nullity and chaos of 'her' land, but with whispers of divine creative power and of a far different land. In the surrounding context, mainly vv. 11a-b and 13-15, the whispers are gently amplified since this smoldering waste and void are yet inhabited even if by desert and demonic beasts.

The Uncanny Kingdom. Kingdom and princes allude to the monarchic period that is the object of much of Isaiah, especially chs. 1–39. This fits with our shadow reading of Israel's story in the poem since the monarchy is the next major stage after the conquest; the latter is alluded to in the imagery of possession and measuring in v. 11. But the end of monarchy in destruction and exile is already contained in the very words that name it: No Kingdom and Nothing Princes. The allusion to kingship and its military power—fortresses and strongholds[70]—continues in the next bicolon, but the power is already past, the fortresses already ruins.

---

68. I am not distinguishing between the absolute אַיִן and the construct form אֵין of the particle in these examples from Isaiah. See Waltke and O'Connor 1990: 661-62 for further examples of the particle's use in the Hebrew Bible.

69. אין שם מלוכה in 34.12 and עד אפס מקום in 5.8.

70. 'Her fortresses' (מבצריה) puns on Bozrah (בצרה).

Thorns and brambles are desert plants that match the desert animals,
the owls, of v. 11. Although using different terminology, they are part
of the motif of briers and thorns that occurs frequently early in the
book.[71] Thorns in fortresses are an inverted image of peace: thorns and
not swords or spears (see 2.4). In the oracle on Damascus, the poet
employs a similar inverted image.

> Damascus ceases to be a city; she has become a heap of ruins; the cities
> of Aroer are deserted.
> They are for flocks who can lie down and no one will disturb them
> (17.1-2).

This passage, 34.11-13b, continues the imbrication of contrasting
images and themes: creation and anticreation, the devastation of Sodom
and Gomorrah (without concern for their evil), destruction and restoration, the wandering in the wilderness and the subsequent conquest,
division and possession of the land including the entire period of the
monarchy. In the Hebrew Bible, life in the land is itself a mix of curse
and blessing for Israel, let alone for the original inhabitants.

> For a brief time your holy people had possession [ירש];
> now our enemies have trampled your holy place (63.18).

By this time in the poem, the violence of vv. 2-8 is gone and replaced
by this eerie picture of unending desolation that yet has life in it and
life lived in a strange community with an equally haunting tranquillity.
This is a perverse image of the remnant, the something that remains
after the divine fury has spent itself. Not only do we have these nightmarish scenes with their latent dream meanings, but as we read this part
of the poem, we encounter imagistic and verbal hints of creation, of
Israel's epic story and of Isaiah's story of a near total, yet ultimately
cleansing, judgment.

> Whoever is left in Zion and remains in Jerusalem will be called Holy,
> everyone who is recorded for life in Jerusalem—once YHWH has washed
> away the vomit of the daughters of Zion and has cleansed the blood-
> stains of Jerusalem from her midst with a judging spirit and with a
> burning spirit (4.3-4).[72]

---

71. שמיר ושית: 5.6, 7.23-25, 9.17, 10.17 and 27.4; קוץ שמיר: 32.13; קוץ: 33.12;
נעצוץ: 7.19 and 55.13; סרפד: 55.13. The lexical variety testifies to Isaiah's encyclopedic quality.

72. The example was not chosen by chance. YHWH's spirit or breath, רוח,
occurs in 34.16; 'judging' is משפט that is in 34.5; and the root for 'burning', בער,

This entire tableau is the shadow side of the Peaceable Kingdom depicted in Isaiah 11; the lexical variety in this passage is another indication of Isaiah's encyclopedic quality.

> The wolf dwells with the lamb and the leopard lies down with the kid,
> the calf, the lion and the fatling all together.[73]
> A small child leads them.
> The cow and the bear graze while their young lie down together; the
> lion[74] eats straw like the ox.
> The nursing infant plays over the asp's hole and the weaned child places
> its hand on the adder's lair.
> They do neither evil nor corruption on my holy mountain
> For the earth is filled with the knowledge of YHWH as the waters cover
> the sea (vv. 6-9).

In both texts animals live at peace with each other. We can extend this to life with humans if we understand Lilith and even the other creatures in 34.14 as human-like, although demonic, figures.

'Shadow reading' and 'shadow side' are yet other attempts to express this mode of reading that is aware of other meanings, allusions and texts, but does not want to make them equal to the manifest reading. This is an uncanny text and an uncanny land. In French 'uncanny' is *l'étrange* and in German, *unheimlich*. I am using the concept to capture the sense of something that is glimpsed or grasped at but not fully or clearly apprehended and of something that is both familiar, homey (German: *Heim*), and strange, alien. This is the hesitation of the fantastic. We read this text with its incredible fury, violence and devastation, and oscillate between a traditional reading that this is only total destruction and condemnation and a shadow reading that glimpses creation, the story of Israel, the remnant and the peaceable kingdom behind or beneath the grim scenes.

---

occurs at the close of v. 9 and is part of the root play on the consonants forming the root.

73. The Greek has a verb in place of 'the fatling'. REB renders: 'the calf and the young lion will feed together'. JPS's translation is similar to mine and has a textual note that 1QIsa[a] and the Septuagint read: 'the calf and the beast of prey shall feed'.

74. Isaiah uses Hebrew synonyms, כפיר, and אריה, for these two occurrences of lion. KJV, NAB and REB translate the synonyms 'young lion' and 'lion' to show the change in words; GNB uses 'lion cubs' and 'lions' while JPS employs 'beast of prey' and 'lion'.

34.13c-15

13c And she is a pasture for jackals,
        grass[75] for ostriches.
14 Demons meet with phantoms,
        and a hairy beast[76] calls to [meets with][77] his friend.
     Indeed there Lilith reposes
        and finds for herself rest.
15 There the owl[78] nests and delivers
        for she hatches and broods[79] in her shade.
     Indeed there vultures[80] gather,
        each with her friend.

For the initial וְהָיְתָה and my translation as 'is', see the previous discussion of v. 9c (p. 61). The initial bicolon is punctuating and transitional; it both emphasizes the previous changes and introduces another group of inhabitants of this eerie land. This closing scene, however, is characterized by life lived in peace and community, a life that shares aspects with Israel's desired life in her land. 32.14-18 is a dreamlike depiction of this life of bounty lived in 'a peaceful pasture' (see 34.13) following the abandonment of 'the fortress' (34.13); it is a depiction that shares much with the one in 35.1-7.

75. This is the usual translation for חָצִיר. However, it is possible to read this as a biform for חָצֵר, 'enclosure' or 'court'; this would form a neater parallel with 'pasture'. 'It shall be the haunt of jackals, an abode for ostriches' (NRSV). 1QIsa^a reads חצצר; Greek and the Targum support either interpretation. See Watson 1984: 43, Wildberger 1982: 1328 and 1354, and Watts 1987: 6-7 for further comments on this and the similar text in 35.7.

76. שָׂעִיר is a pun on שֵׂעִיר, Seir, Edom's byname (21.11). Since Esau is the ancestor of Edom, in our shadow reading 'his friend' can be Jacob/Israel.

77. See Wildberger 1982: 1328 for discussion of this alternate translation that reflects the meaning of 'to meet' for קרא, whether or not we see a different verbal root. יקרא is the only *yiqtol* form in a series of *qatal*s in vv. 13-15.

78. See the note on v. 11. Others see this as a tree snake or arrow snake, e.g. Watts 1987: 4, 6; JPS; and Wildberger 1982: 1325, 1328-29.

79. 'Brood' is taken in the sense of watching over and protecting. This is a guess at the meaning of דגר which occurs only one other time in the Hebrew Bible in Jer. 17.11 where a partridge hatches or broods without having given birth.

80. The term, דַּיָּה, occurs elsewhere only in Deut. 14.13 in a list of unclean birds. 'Vultures', in my translation, make a fitting closure to the description of 'her' inhabitants which begins in v. 11 with the desert owl, קָאַת, that also occurs in the Deuteronomy list (Deut. 14.17).

The fortress is deserted, the noisy city abandoned;
Both hill and tower are now dens forever, the joy of asses, forage for flocks
Until a spirit is poured out on us from on high
And the wilderness becomes farm land and farm land is thought of as a forest.
Justice [מִשְׁפָּט] dwells in the wilderness and righteousness lives in the farm land.
The work of righteousness is peace and the effect of righteousness is unending calm and security.
My people live in *a peaceful pasture*, in secure dwellings and quiet resting places.

In our poem, attention is riveted on the desolate land by the thrice repeated 'there', שָׁם, that is intensified by 'indeed' (אַך) in 34.14c and by the locative -*āh* in 15a. This recalls the name 'There is not *There* a Kingdom' and details what, in fact, is there.

The desolate land provides pasture and grass for jackals and ostriches, two more types of wild animals living outside human society (13.22). At another time, however, they both honor YHWH as a sign of the wondrous new thing he does.

I am doing something new: right now it is sprouting, don't you perceive it?
I am putting a road in the wilderness, rivers in the barrens.[81]
Wild animals honor me, *jackals and ostriches*,
Because I place water in the wilderness, rivers in the barrens
To give drink to my chosen people (43.19-20).

Imagery of a road and water in the wilderness anticipates the transformation in the second part of our poem (35.1-10). תַּנִּים, jackals, mimics תַּנִּין, the sea monster or dragon defeated at the time of creation and cited by Isaiah as an indication of YHWH's power to save (27.1; 51.9).

The encounter of demons (צִיִּים) and phantoms (אִיִּים) is mirrored in the word-play. צִיִּים also puns on Zion (צִיּוֹן: 34.8; 35.10) and thirsty (צִיָּה: 35.1). We move now from recognizable animals into the realm of mythic or demonic creatures[82] and their peaceful existence. They meet

81. I translate יְשִׁימוֹן as 'barrens' to distinguish it from 'desert', עֲרָבָה, in 35.1 and 6.

82. See Wildberger 1982: 1328, 1347-49 for these translations and this interpretation of the creatures as demonic. Watts 1987: 13 agrees with Wildberger. Other translations differ on their rendering of the three creatures: 'wildcats, hyenas and

and call to one another. We also move from male animals, beginning in v. 6, to females who inhabit 'her' land. Verses 13c-14b include one female group, literally 'daughters of ostriches',[83] while 14c-15d are all females. 'His friend' of 14b modulates to 'her friend' at the end of v. 15. This inclusion of male and female is characteristic of Isaiah, most noticeable in the focus on Jacob/Israel (male) and then on Zion/Jerusalem (female).[84]

Lilith can be a night demonness since her name is similar to the Hebrew word for night, or she is a storm demonness in parallel with a Mesopotamian demonness (Watts 1987: 13-14; Wildberger 1982: 1347-49).[85] NJB, NRSV, Watts and Wildberger all render this as a proper name 'Lilith'; JPS and NAB as 'the lilith' and the others variously as 'night creatures' (NIV), 'night monster' (GNB) and 'the nightjar' (REB). All of the latter gloss over the fact that this is a woman.[86]

In any case Lilith is singular, an individual woman, and not a plural group as the preceding creatures in vv. 6-14b. Other than YHWH, she is the only named individual in the poem; the other proper names are for lands, Edom and Lebanon, or cities, Bozrah and Zion. She lies down and 'finds for herself rest'. Rest (מנוח) intones other texts that speak of peace and security, for example, Ps. 116.7 and Ruth 3.1, or its lack, for example, Deut. 28.65 and Lam. 1.3. It also refers to the related noun 'rest' (מנוחה) that can denote the land of Israel as a place of rest (Deut. 12.9; Ps. 95.11). In Isaiah it is a resting place for humans (28.12) and

goat-demons' (NRSV; JPS; NIV similar) and 'wild cats, hyenas and satyrs' (NJB; NAB similar).

83. Daughters of...' and not just 'ostrich' is the normal expression: Lev. 11.16; Deut. 14.15; Isa. 13.21; and 43.20.

84. This includes the contrast, noted previously, between the king of Babylon and Lady Babylon (see above, pp. 58-60).

85. Both Watts and Wildberger briefly trace how Lilith, beginning with this sole reference in the Hebrew Bible, developed in both Judaic and Christian traditions. See Scholem's section on 'Lilith' in *EncJud*, XI: 245-50 for discussion and bibliography.

86. Sawyer first drew my attention to the significance of Lilith as a proper name for a woman in his comment on the NRSV's translation. 'The appearance of "Lilith" here is very significant. In popular Jewish and Christian tradition, Lilith was Adam's first wife, who unlike submissive Eve escaped from his chauvinistic domination, and has haunted society, threatening male institutions, including marriage, ever since. Today she is a popular model for radical feminists—there is even a journal of Jewish feminism published in New York under the title *Lilith*' (1995: 155).

for God (66.1). In 32.18, cited above and related to 35.1-10, the poet states 'my people live in a peaceful pasture, in secure dwellings and quiet resting places [מנוחת]' (see p. 83). These parallels continue to remind us that this is a perverse remnant living in this desolate land.

Verse 15a-b is remarkable, in this poem, for its series of four verbs, none with a direct object; this accentuates the action. The first two are in a *qatal-wayyiqtol* sequence that is perfective; it highlights the act itself, not the process, and in addition expresses the fact that nesting and delivering are a regular event.[87] To nest (קָנַן) or make a nest (קֵן) echoes גנן, to protect or deliver (31.5; 37.35; 38.6), and the related noun, garden (גן or גנה: 51.3; 61.11).[88] A garden can be a site for fertility worship (1.29; 66.17) and an image of destruction, 'a garden without water' (1.30).[89] It is a grand image of restoration since Zion can be 'like Eden...like the garden of YHWH' (51.3) and the people 'like a well-watered garden' (58.11). The translation 'to deliver' reflects the ambiguity of מלט which means both to save or rescue (31.5) and to give birth to (66.7).[90] Protection, security and restoration are all latent themes of the bicolon.

'To hatch' is the denotation of the piel of בקע in 59.5; the qal refers to the breaking forth of water (35.6; 48.21; 63.12) and of light (58.8) in contexts of guidance and abundance. Shade and shadow, צל, in addition, are safety and shelter from the blazing sun (4.6; 25.4); YHWH hides and protects his servant in the shadow of his hand (49.2; 51.16). The second two verbs, 'hatches and broods' are both *weqatal* and I take them as *waw-copulatives* that make an epexegetical comment, introduced by 'for' in my translation, spelling out the activity of the first colon (see above, p. 38).

In v. 15c-d the gathering of vultures, females, each with her friend, mirrors the meeting of the demons, males, who call each to his friend. Meeting and gathering serve to enclose this scene of life in the demonic

87. This is the sole *wayyiqtol* form in the poem; *weyiqtols* occur in 35.1-6. For initial discussion of Hebrew verb forms with waw, see p. 38.

88. For further discussion of Isaiah's use of גנן and גן, see Miscall 1993: 80, 92-93.

89. The passage in 1.29-30 was already noted in relation to the image of withering in 34.4 (see p. 41).

90. For other Isaianic usages of מלט see 20.6; 46.2, 4 and 49.24-25. The verb can occur without a direct object: Isa. 46.4; Amos 2.15; Pss. 33.17 and 107.20. The objects in Isa. 34.15 are either her young or herself in the sense that she finds a secure place for herself.

world (vv. 13c-15d), a life which uncannily and mutely witnesses to Israel's dreams of life in the restored land. The scene concludes the first major part of our poem that depicts the divine destruction and its aftermath in an impressionistic, yet literal, style. It is literal as opposed to figurative; with the exception of v. 4, there are no similes or other overt figures of speech. It is impressionistic since the poet proceeds by putting together scenes and images that both complement and clash with each other; his landscape is not deployed in a tight logical or narrative mode.

The Scroll

34.16-17

16   Seek from the scroll of YHWH and read:
        Not one of these is missing![91]
     [Each with her friend, they do not decide
        because 'my mouth', it has commanded][92]
     and his breath, it has gathered them.

91.   For this sense of missing or lacking for נעדר, see 40.26 and 59.15.

92.   The bracketed text, v. 16c, is obscure and probably corrupt. I do not attempt any emendations and my translation reflects the MT. I feel that it is seriously misleading, especially in a detailed study such as this, to offer an emended text that I would not want to defend as the original or best text.

אשה רעותה are the final words of v. 15 and the first words of v. 16c where they may be a dittography or scribal gloss. On the other hand, the repetition can be a deliberate way of tying v. 16 to the preceding. In 15c-d the word order is 'they gathered, vultures [feminine plural], each with her friend' while in 16c, it is 'each with her friend...his spirit, it gathered them [feminine plural]'. However we understand this obscure line, I think it is clear that, on one level, it is referring directly back to v. 15.

In Isaiah פקד means to punish, to determine one's fate (10.12; 13.11; 23.17; 24.22), to deposit (10.28) and to muster (13.4); this range of meanings forms a parallel with צוה, to command, and קבץ, to gather. In the niphal פקד means to be missed in Num. 31.49 and Judg. 21.3; this meaning is similar to נעדר in Isa. 34.16b. Such a range of meaning for this one root does enrich our reading, but it does not help to clarify the text. My translation is based on context as much as the term itself; the sense is that they don't decide and act on their own to determine their fate since YHWH's mouth and spirit have decided the state of affairs.

'My mouth' renders פי. The first person echoes v. 5 but is otherwise out of place in this verse; 'his spirit' follows. פי can be a construct which would likewise not fit the context. Based on 1QIsa[a] and the Greek, Wildberger (1982: 1329-30) emends to read 'the mouth of YHWH' and points to parallels in 1.20, 40.5 and 58.14. This forms a fit parallel for the following 'his spirit'.

17   And it has cast for them the lot,
           and his hand has divided her for them with the line.
       Forever they will possess her,
           for generation to generation they will dwell in her.

The poem opened with the call of the nations and the earth to witness
divine wrath falling on themselves. We, both ancient and modern
readers, have stood apart to hear, read and see with the nations and the
earth or land what befalls them. We read, as it were, looking over their
shoulders. However, the imperatives 'Seek!' and 'Read!', both masculine plural, have no named addressees in the text and they are therefore
addressed to the nations, to any who can hear and read, and even to us,
the readers, who, although outside the text, are invited to enter into the
text. These imperatives without addressees are analogous to the many
pronouns without specific antecedents, pronouns that occur in vv. 16-
17. The imperatives, therefore, preserve and augment the mysterious
atmosphere of the poem by opening it to unspecified hearers and readers; this will continue in the pronouns and imperatives in 35.1-4.

They, the unnamed addressees, and we are directed to the scroll of
YHWH, a multilevel image alluding to the scroll written by YHWH
(Exod. 32.32-33) and the scroll of the covenant written by Moses
(Exod. 24.4-7), to the Hebrew Scriptures or some portion of them, to
the scroll of Isaiah (Isa. 29.11-12, 18; 30.8) and to the shriveled heavens of this poem (34.4). The entire preceding and following description
of land and inhabitants is contained in the scroll: not one part or one
creature is missing. Verses 16-17 are transitional, looking both back-
ward and forward; all the scenes of our poem are in the scroll however
we conceive of it.

This is a common interpretation which focuses on the contents of the
scroll and their accord with the contents of Isaiah 34–35. Watts offers
an added twist to this interpretation by directing attention to the written
scroll in his translation of the first part of the contested portion of v. 16:

           Examine YHWH's scroll and read aloud.
               Let nothing be left out.
                   Let (no line) miss its parallel line (1987: 4).

In addition, the verse is a reminder, within the poem itself, that the
poem is a written work and perhaps itself the scroll, or part of the
scroll, of YHWH. However we understand the verse, it is (re)asserting
that this is YHWH's work: he—his mouth, his breath and his hand—has

commanded, gathered and apportioned. The assertion is necessary in part because of the absence of YHWH in vv. 9-15 and the indirect references to his actions in vv. 1-8 and in 35.1-10. However, even this assertion of divine power substitutes his scroll, mouth, breath and hand for YHWH himself. The latter three are frequent symbols of YHWH at different points in Isaiah.[93] I translate רוּחַ as 'breath', and not 'spirit' or even 'wind', to match the body imagery of 'mouth' and 'hand'. This imagery was already introduced in the 'corpses, 'blood', 'fat' and 'innards' of vv. 3-7 and it is added to in 35.3-6 and 10.

The pronoun הוא occurs three times in vv. 16-17 and I translate 'it', although it is 'he' in most translations. 'It' better captures the fact that it is YHWH's mouth or breath, and not YHWH himself, acting. The breath that gathers 'them' (feminine plural) at the close of v. 16 also casts the lot 'for them' (feminine plural) at the opening of v. 17.[94] 'Cast the lot' refers to the processes of making a decision or deciding someone's fate and of dividing up the land. 'To cast' is the hiphil of 'to fall', נפל, which echoes 'to wither', נבל, and the descending sword and animals. The grim scenes of the poem are much in evidence.

On the other hand, casting the lot, גורל, alludes to the procedure of dividing up the land among the tribes as described in Num. 26.55-56, Josh. 14.2 and 19.51. Again, we encounter the double reading of a nightmare and of a dream, of the demonic land and of the land of Israel, both antecedents of the reiterated 'her' in 17c-d. The first 'for them' (feminine plural) refers to the preceding female creatures in vv. 13-15; the second (masculine plural) refers both back and forward to the male creatures, including humans. The bicolon can be rendered:

> And it has cast for the women the lot,
> and his hand has divided her for the men with the line.

The temporal phrases and two verbs in 17c-d, ירשׁ and שׁכן, parallel those in vv. 10-11. The bicolon echoes the desolation of 34.7-15 and anticipates the restoration of 35.1-10. In 11a-b the two verbs refer to possession of the desolate land by the desert owls; that bicolon is followed immediately by the image of stretching the line and the weights

---

93. For example, mouth: 1.20; 40.5; 55.11; 62.2. Breath, spirit or wind (רוח): 11.2; 30.1; 32.15; 40.7; 44.3; 61.1. Hand(s): 1.25; 11.11, 15; 23.11; 40.2; 45.11-12; 59.1; 66.2.

94. In a difficult text in 66.18 YHWH comes 'to gather all nations and tongues'; see below, pp. 128-30.

that produce or measure the land of chaos. In v. 17 the order of possession and measurement is reversed and the powerful images of chaos
removed. The change is indicated in part by the lexical shift from 'line'
and 'weights' to 'lot' and 'line'. I translate these two final verbs—both
yiqtol—with the future tense to contrast them with the preceding six
qatal forms, translated with the present or the perfect, in 16b-17b (see
below, p. 91, for an alternate rendering). 'They', who have multiple
identifications, possess and dwell in 'her' forever.

The Nightmare and the Dream: A Transition. Reading the two verses as
a transition within the poem rather than as the conclusion to an independent poem in ch. 34 involves seeing the nightmarish and dream
aspects in 34.1-15 and 35.1-10 on an equal footing, rather than in a
chronological or narrative relation of past judgment and present or
future salvation. And in the last part of our poem, 35.1-10, the dream is
the manifest meaning and the nightmare the latent; the dominant picture of transformation and restoration will be disturbed and unsettled by
the shadows of divine wrath and the demonic realm. In a sense the two
parts of the poem present the same scenario. To use photographic
imagery, one part of the poem is the negative and the other is the positive print; as usual, I leave it open as to which is which.

The Dream

35.1-2

1   Let wilderness and dry land rejoice;[95]
        desert, shout and bloom;
2a   Like the crocus,[96] let her bloom luxuriantly;

95. יְשֻׂשׂוּם is a difficult form because of the suffixed *mem*. Watts, in a textual
note (1987: 6-7), translates 'will be glad in them' in which the suffix, taken as the
third person masculine plural object 'them', refers to the preceding description of
the land. The deserts rejoice in the grim fates of the land and its inhabitants. This is
a possible reading that can be combined, in our reading, with the fact that the latent,
positive underside of the earlier scenes is elating the deserts. The final *mem* can also
be a reflexive pronoun as in Watts's main translation: 'they rouse themselves in
gladness'. Others see the *mem* as a dittography of the following *mem* of מִדְבָּר or as
an original *paragogic nun* adapted to this following *mem*; see Wildberger 1982:
1353 for discussion. I tend toward the latter understanding and therefore do not
reflect the *mem* in my translation.

96. With NRSV and Watts (1987: 4). JPS translates 'a rose' but notes 'a crocus'
as the literal meaning. See Wildberger 1982: 1353 for possible identifications; he

b   let her shout, shout aloud,[97] yea, sing!
c   The glory of the Lebanon is given to her,
d   the splendor of the Carmel and the Sharon.
e   They see the glory of YHWH,
            the splendor of our God.

The second major part of our poem opens with two closely related bicola, perhaps a quatrain, similar to 34.1. In addition, I translate the five *yiqtol* verbs as jussives (Waltke and O'Connor 1990: 570; REB; NJB) and include the piel infinitive (רבן) at the close of 2b in this meaning. The second, third and fifth verbs are *weyiqtol*s occurring after a preceding *yiqtol* and continuing the jussive meaning. Jussives recall the imperatives that opened the poem. Other translations such as NRSV, NIV and JPS translate as future, 'will/shall be glad', or as a present, for example, Watts: 'rouse themselves...rejoices' (1987: 4). However, as I commented previously, differences in tense and mode, while necessary in an English translation, are all contained in the one Hebrew form regardless of which meaning may be dominant in a given context.

The initial verb follows immediately upon the preceding verb that closes 34.17; there is no intervening waw or other connective particle. In other words, minus the chapter and verse numbers, there is no significant break between 34.17 and 35.1. This is the way it is presented in my initial presentation of the entire poem, although a break is supplied in the present context. The following text offsets the split and I translate with present tenses to highlight the connection, to stress the immediacy of the scene and to reflect the multiple tenses that can be used to translate the Hebrew verbs. The antecedents of 'they' occur both before and after this passage.

> Forever they possess her,
>   for generation to generation they dwell in her.
> They rejoice, wilderness and dry land,
>   desert shouts and blooms.

translates 'lilies'. The line division reflects a transference of the line end, the Silluq and Sof Pasuq in the MT, to after the preceding verb as in *BHS*.

97. 'Bloom luxuriantly' is Waltke and O'Connor's rendering of the first use of the cognate internal accusative (1990: 167 n. 38; GKC 117q), while 'shout aloud' is my translation of the second such construction. I take גילת to be either a noun or a feminine infinitive construct; it would be a construct before a connective waw, perhaps to avoid the hiatus of *-āh wᵉra-* (GKC 130b). 'Shout, shout aloud' reflects the emphatic particle אף which comes between the verb and the cognate accusative.

Wilderness, dry land and desert all explicitly intone, in a positive mode, Israel's exodus and wilderness traditions that were latent in the first part of the poem; now, in the second part, these positive themes are the manifest meaning while the imagery of desolation becomes latent. I note that the wilderness narratives and traditions are themselves multivalent and ambiguous. This is a time of wandering, suffering and death for Israel, but it is also a time of leadership by both YHWH and Moses, of divine revelation and of divine sustenance. Our mode of shadow reading now unsettles the glory and joy of these scenes in ch. 35 with glimpses of the violence and destruction that underlie and surround them. The dream is not a simple wish fulfilment or fantasy since it is filled with glimpses and traces of the violence and devastation that both precede it and now surround it.

Most commentaries approach the two parts of the poem, often two independent poems for them, by putting them in a chronological framework in which the destruction, the judgment, of ch. 34 precedes the transformation and return of ch. 35. Indeed, the judgment of ch. 34 can be seen as the necessary prelude to the salvation of ch. 35; the wicked (the nations) are destroyed and the righteous (Israel) saved. Thus ch. 34 is behind us once we move into ch. 35. However, my mode of reading, with its emphasis on a plural text and on the presence of latent meanings and shadow readings, recognizes this possibility but also maintains the entire poem as a depiction of simultaneous scenes. Wrath and destruction stand side by side with joy and restoration. In a chronological or narrative reading, we can start with either, that is, we can read ch. 35 before ch. 34 just as easily as the reverse. This regards the two parts of the poem as forming a true diptych and takes the artistic metaphor more literally to the extent that the nightmare and the dream are envisioned as painted on two juxtaposed panels, without dominance or preference given to either.

ציה puns on Zion, ציון (34.8; 35.10), and ערבה is yet another term involved in the root play of ב, ר and ע (see above, p. 30 n. 2 and p. 73). Wilderness, מדבר, in particular, is polyvalent in its references to restoration (32.15-16; 40.3; 41.18-19; 51.3), to the display of divine power by turning rivers into desert (50.2) and to the desolation of the world (14.17), of the city (27.10) and of Zion (64.9). I cite 32.15-16 again because of its relevance to this context.

The wilderness becomes farm land [כרמל][98] and farm land is thought of
as a forest.
Justice [משפט] dwells in the wilderness and righteousness lives in the
farm land.

The eerie silence of the demonic land yields to songs and shouts
while the thorns are replaced by the flourishing crocus; the latter, 'like
the crocus', is one of the two similes in the latter part of the poem
(35.6a; see my previous comments on 34.4, p. 45). The initial two
bicola slow our reading through the use of waws and repetition. The
next bicolon (2c-d), however, proceeds with only one waw and without
repetition, yet the line still has a solemnity that matches its content, the
continuing transformation of the desert and of the demonic land. The
latter is included in our poem through the ambiguous 'to her' which
matches the polyvalent 'she' and 'her' of 34.9-17; the demonic land is,
at once, the desolate earth, wasted Edom, Zion and Israel, Sodom and
Gomorrah and Babylon that are all part of the transformation.

Unlike other commentators, I see no reason to limit this vision of
restoration to Israel alone. As already noted, McKenzie states 'salvation
as envisaged here is for Israel alone' (1968: 12). Wildberger and Watts
are not so explicit but speak with the assumption that ch. 35 is about
Israel's renewal and salvation. Seitz contrasts chs. 34 and 35: 'The vio-
lator Edom goes from fat to "no kingdom". The desolated Israel blos-
soms again' (1993: 239). One major result of my reading is that the
poem in Isaiah 34–35 does not support such clear and exclusive contrasts. Restoration can be just as general as destruction.

Glory, כבוד, and splendor, הדר, emphasize the visual realm of light.
In Isaiah, both, particularly 'glory', mean, first, grand and even fear-
some appearance (4.2; 62.2).

> Go into the rock caves and into hollows in the dust—
> From the terror of YHWH and from his dread splendor when he rises to
> terrorize the earth (2.19).

> Holy, Holy, Holy! O YHWH Hosts!
> The whole earth is filled with his glory! (6.3).

Secondly, they mean wealth and nobility (8.7; 61.3), 'my people go
into exile without knowledge; their nobles [כבודם] are dying of hunger'

---

98. The common noun means farmland, garden or orchard; as a proper name,
whether definite or not, it refers to the Carmel, fertile hill country along the coast
for about 15 miles north of Mt Carmel. The Carmel is referred to in 35.2.

(5.13). And thirdly, they mean manifest presence, especially YHWH's (3.8; 63.1).

> The moon will pale and the sun be ashamed for YHWH of hosts is king
> In Mount Zion and in Jerusalem: Glorious before his elders (24.23).[99]

> The glory of YHWH is revealed and all flesh sees it together (40.5).

With the exception of YHWH and Zion (vv. 2 and 10) (that were mentioned in the first part of the poem), Lebanon, Carmel and Sharon[100] are the last proper names in the poem to be added to the short list of such names: YHWH, Edom, Bozrah, Zion and Lilith. Individually the three place names connote height, power and beauty in both positive (14.8; 65.10) and negative registers (2.13; 37.24). 'The glory of Lebanon comes to you... to beautify my holy place' (60.13); 'he hacks down the thickets of the forest with an ax and the Lebanon, in its majesty, topples' (10.34). Their desolation is described in a passage already cited for its use of עבר, 'to pass by', and for its scene of general destruction.

> Listen! The valiant[101] cry aloud in the streets; messengers of peace
> bitterly weep.
> Highways are deserted; those who pass by on the road have ceased.
> A covenant is broken; cities rejected; humanity disregarded.
> The earth wilts, it languishes; Lebanon pales and withers;
> The Sharon is like the desert; Bashan and Carmel are stripped bare
> (33.7-9).[102]

The first part of the passage was cited previously in regard to the phrase 'those who pass by' and its parallel in 34.10d. The passage anticipates the withering and the desolation of the first section of our

---

99. In the satire of the king of Babylon in ch. 14, 'glory' ironically refers to the 'grave'. 'All the kings of the nations, all of them, lie in "glory", each in his house [tomb]' (v. 18).

100. See p. 92 n. 98 for the Carmel. The Sharon is a coastal plain extending about 30 miles south from Mt Carmel. The Lebanon is the coastal mountain range that extends for approximately 100 miles north of Israel. It was noted for its height and for its cedar forests (see 1 Kgs 4.33 and Ps. 104.16).

101. This is NRSV's rendering that ultimately derives from Delitzsch; it is a conjecture. NIV and REB are similar. JPS, citing 'a few manuscripts', translates 'the Arielites' reflecting 'Ariel' in 29.1-2, an apparent title for Jerusalem. NAB and JPS are similar. See Watts (1985: 422) and Wildberger (1982: 1294) for a discussion of the attempts to understand the Hebrew term.

102. See above, p. 73.

poem, the desolation that, on one level of reading, is being transformed in this section of our poem.

The transformation happens. The poet does not even indirectly ascribe this process to YHWH's action. Glory *is given* to her; however, previously, YHWH *gave* the nations to slaughter (34.2). The poet continues the vague and enigmatic quality of the poem in the use of pronouns. 'They', who see the glory of YHWH, are highlighted by the use of the pleonastic pronoun המה that is yet another pronoun with diverse possible antecedents. 'They' can variously be the wilderness, the Lebanon, and so on, that are being beautified in the immediate context; the creatures of 34.11-15; the nations of 34.1-8; and the others alluded to in the latent, shadow aspects of the demonic land, especially the inhabitants of Zion/Israel.

Seeing—an explicit theme here—was intoned explicitly in 'Look!' (הנה) in 34.5 and implicitly in the impressive imagery of the first half of our poem. Now divine glory is seen, not a divine sword. Natural glory and splendor are given to 'her', but 'they' see the glory and splendor of YHWH, 'our' God. The natural splendor can be given to another, but 'My [YHWH] glory I don't give to another' (42.8). The poet leaves us to muse on the possible relations between the glory and splendor of nature and of divinity: Identity? Sharp contrast such as that between the transient and the lasting or the lesser and the greater?

The bicolon in 2e-f is framed by 'they' and 'our'; the frame underlines the contrast between 'they' and 'we' without indicating who these two groups are. Developing the relationships of individuals or groups who are identified only by pronouns and not deciding for one set of specific identities for them was first suggested to me by Clines in his 1976 study of the servant song in 52.13–53.12. Such an approach accords nicely with my open, expansive mode of reading and is a way that would enrich the reading of many other parts of Isaiah. I discuss one of the prevalent pronouns in the vision.

Who is 'We'? I use the singular verb and put 'we' in quotation marks to highlight the fact that I am dealing with 'we' (and 'they') first and foremost as a textual and grammatical category in this poem and in the entire book of Isaiah, and not as a reference to an actual historical group or even to a single identifiable group in the vision of Isaiah. The impact of this tactic will become clear as we progress. In the context of the poem, 'we', at first and in most interpretations, is the poet referring to YHWH-God while speaking loosely for Israel or for some group in Israel, for example, the righteous (33.13-16), that he identifies with. In a strong variation of this reading, 'we' is Israel or this righteous group asserting its voice in the poem, shunting the poet aside, similar to YHWH's interruption in 34.5. A third possibility is that 'we' is a heavenly chorus, the righteous counterpart of the destroyed heavenly armies (34.4; 6.1-8; 40.1-11). This is a weak alternative since there is no parallel for it in the poem. I will discuss other possibilities after the following digression on 'we'.

The issue of the 'we', the first person plural voice that speaks at points throughout the book—for example, 1.9, 9.5, 33.22, 40.8 and 63.7-64.11—is important to a reading of Isaiah. I already introduced and briefly commented on the larger question of speakers in the book of Isaiah in relation to the opening call to the nations in 34.1 (see above, p. 35). Watts helped sharpen the focus on speakers for me by treating all of Isaiah as a grand drama which he divides into separate statements or speeches with the speaker, whether an individual or a group and whether named ('Yahweh' in 34.5) or not ('Judean Chorus' in 35.1-2), indicated in the left margin. This narrows the issue, first, because it focuses on who is speaking to whom within the vision of Isaiah and not on some putative ancient historical setting. Secondly, it demonstrates, often in direct contrast with Watts's claims, that Isaiah can be read as a plural text by renaming many of the speakers and by redefining the extent of many of the speeches that he indicates. This includes my frequent practice, in evidence in this reading, of leaving many of these decisions, including the related questions of who is spoken to and who is spoken about, open in terms of the several alternatives that can exist.

Conrad gave a specific twist to the topic by devoting an entire chapter to the question: 'Who Are "We"?' (1991: 83-116). He begins with a consideration of 42.24 with its clear distinction of 'we' and 'they'.

> Who gave up Jacob for plunder and Israel to those preying upon him?
> Was it not YHWH whom *we* have sinned against?
> *They* were not willing to walk in his roads; they would not hear his teaching.

He maintains that the 'we' represents the implied audience of the book of Isaiah, that is, the group of survivors or the righteous remnant that the vision is addressed to. The 'we' and 'they' contrast in 42.24 'suggests that the implied audience is part of a community divided into a "we" (the implied community) and a "they" (a rival faction)' (Conrad 1991: 83).

> Through the first person plural voice the implied audience, a community of survivors, is incorporated into the world of the text. It emerges as a character with a speaking voice, as does Hezekiah. The beginning and end of the book are closely related because the 'we', which speaks of itself in the beginning as a community of survivors having experienced the devastating judgment of the Lord, foreshadows the way the Lord speaks about the community of survivors at the end of the book (Conrad 1991: 116).

Conrad's treatment is insightful, but it can be extended and complicated. The initial statement that 'we' are a remnant, a group of survivors left from the destruction, is immediately followed by the prophet's denunciation of them for their evil; 'we' becomes 'you' (masculine plural). Being a remnant doesn't necessarily mean being righteous.

> If YHWH of hosts had not left *us* a few survivors, *we* would have become
>   like Sodom, *we* would have resembled Gomorrah.
> Hear the word of YHWH, you rulers of Sodom!
> Give ear to the teaching of our God, you people of Gomorrah!
> What to me is the multitude of your sacrifices? says YHWH (1.9-10).

Peoples and nations can say 'we' in a righteous, not just an arrogant, mode. 'Let *us* go up to the mountain of YHWH…that he may teach *us* his ways and that *we* may walk in his paths' (2.2). Faced with this declaration on the part of the nations, a voice exhorts Jacob to do likewise. 'O house of Jacob, come, let *us* walk in the light of YHWH!' (2.5). 'We' can be like 'they' even if the latter are the nations. Israelite sinners can say 'we'.

> Sinners in Zion are frightened; trembling has seized the godless:
> 'Who of us can live with a devouring fire?
> Who of us can live with an everlasting blaze?' (33.14).

They are immediately informed that proper behavior will allow them to dwell there.

> Those who walk righteously and speak honestly, who despise getting profit from oppression, who hold their hands back from taking a bribe, who close their ears to proposals of bloodshed and who shut their eyes to sights of evil: they will dwell on heights; their refuge will be rock fortresses (33.15-16).

However, at another point 'we' confess that 'justice is far from us, and righteousness does not reach us' (59.9). They employ the pair 'YHWH' and 'our God'.

> We wait for justice, and there is none; for victory, and it is far from us.
> For many are our crimes before you and our sin testifies against us;
> Indeed our crimes are with us and we know well our iniquities:
> Transgressing, and denying YHWH, and turning back from following *our God*,
> Speaking oppression and revolt, conceiving and muttering lying words from the heart (vv. 11-13).

In a subsequent proclamation of sin and a plea for help in 63.7–64.11, the initial voice is first person singular, who then speaks of Israel as 'they' in reference to the past and as 'we' in reference to the present. To put it simply, 'they', the ancestors, sinned and 'we' now suffer. Living in the present amid burned ruins is part of the misery. (This distinction between ancestors and present-day people is also applicable to 42.24; Conrad's divided-community interpretation is not the only possible reading.)

> I bring to mind the kindnesses of YHWH, YHWH's acts for which he is praised,
> Because of all that YHWH has done for *us* and the great good for the *house of Israel*,
> That he has done for *them* in his compassion, in his great kindnesses...
> In his love and in his compassion he redeemed them; he lifted them and carried them all the days of old.
> They revolted and tormented his holy spirit. And he became an enemy to them; he fought against them...
> Although for a short while your holy people were in possession, *our* enemies now trample your sanctuary.
> For a long time *we* have been those you don't rule over, those who aren't called by your name (63.7-10, 18-19).

These few examples demonstrate that 'we' can be used by a variety of speakers, and that when it is used by Israel it can be used to refer to Israel as either righteous or sinful. Conrad's distinction between 'we', the righteous survivors, and 'they', the oppressive, wicked survivors, is still possible, but it is no longer the only way to read these passages or other analogous parts of the book of Isaiah. 'We' and 'they' aren't always clear and distinct categories that stand in sharp opposition. 'We' can be 'they'.

To return to our poem, 'they' who see the divine glory can say 'our

God'. The speakers who say 'our God' can be Israel but now with the emphasis on their continued admission of guilt and on their having to live with 'an everlasting blaze' (33.14: עולם; see 34.10, 17) and amid burned ruins (64.10: חרבה; see 34.10). In this sense and in our mode of shadow reading, 'our God' can be uttered not only by remnant Israel but also by the perverse remnant composed of Lilith and the other creatures living in the blasted land of unending ruin and fire. Since Israel can call YHWH 'our father' and 'our redeemer' (63.16; 64.7) while still in misery, we do not have to posit the fact that these creatures are themselves experiencing the restoration, only that they are witnessing it and commenting on it. This is analogous to the utterance of 'our God' immediately following a declaration of human transience.

> A voice says, 'Cry!' And he said, 'What shall I cry?'
> All flesh is grass and all its goodness like a wildflower.
> Grass dries, a flower withers when YHWH's wind blows on it'—
> Surely the people are grass!
> Grass dries, a flower withers, but the word of *our God* stands forever
>   (40.6-8).

Finally, 'we' is we, the readers, ancient and modern, who are invited to insert ourselves into the poem, to be no longer content to just look over the shoulders of others. Whether we, actual readers as a group or as individuals, respond to this invitation and say 'our God' depends on whether or not we accept and identify with YHWH as he appears in this poem and on how we understand this acceptance. Most commentators want to accept, at least to some extent, this YHWH as 'our God', but are troubled by the violence and destruction of the first part of the poem. This desire, coupled with this troubling, explains in large part their attempts to lessen or remove this disturbing aspect by justifying YHWH's actions as merited judgment or by reducing the impact of the descriptions by historicizing them. I discussed these attempts at some length in a previous digression on the justice of this judgment (see above, pp. 63-69). In this approach we the readers can say 'our God' if this God fits with our concepts of what a just and saving God should be.

On the other hand we the readers can enter the poem on its own terms which is what I have been attempting to do in this reading. Since the poem is a powerful and fluctuating combination of violence and tranquillity, of desert and sown, of nightmare and dream and of fantasy and horror, to enter it on its own terms is not a simple undertaking. Since YHWH is connected with both violent rage and vibrant restoration and is, at the same time, kept in the background as the indirect and muted actor, to say 'our God' is not a simple affirmation. Who is 'our God' within this poem? What does he do or not do? How and why does he act?

35.3-4

3   Strengthen weak hands
        and faltering knees firm up;[103]
4   Say to trembling hearts:
        Be strong! Do not fear!
    See! Your God!
        Vengeance comes!
    Divine retaliation!
        It comes and saves you![104]

With 'seek' and 'read' in 34.16, this is the second series of imperatives in the poem with unspecified speaker(s) and addressees. All of the imperatives, including the initial calls to the nations in 34.1, are masculine plural. I extend the polysemy of those who utter 'our God' to those who exhort others to strengthen the weak and assume that whoever says 'our God' then issues these proclamations. I employ 'it' for pleonastic הוא in 4f to reflect the impersonal style that emphasizes the retaliation and not God himself. In Hebrew, however, הוא can mean both 'he' and 'it'. In accord with the stress on the immediacy of the vision, I use the present tense rather than the future that is used in most translations.

Finally, translations such as the JPS, NIV and NRSV enclose the exhortation to the trembling hearted within quotation marks so that v. 4b-f, in my scansion, is addressed to them.

---

103. The bicolon is enclosed by the two piel imperatives and has a chiastic structure: verb—noun phrase—noun phrase—verb (Watson 1984: 204). The structure is reflected in the translation and the enclosure is marked by the use of a period. The same structure occurs in 35.5.

104. The final term, וְיֹשַׁעֲכֶם, is a difficult form because of the 'a' vowel with *shin*; it is to be read as a hiphil imperfect with a pronominal suffix (GKC 65f). Commentators have variously suggested changes in vocalization to produce a different verb form, a noun or a participle. A noun or participle that would produce something like 'your savior' would balance 'your God' that opens the two bicola. I agree with Watts who reads it as a verb; 'its meaning is clear, even if its form is unusual' (1987: 7). Wildberger (1982: 1353-54) comes to a similar conclusion.

> Say to those with fearful hearts,
>   'Be strong, do not fear;
> your God will come,
>   he will come with vengeance;
> with divine retribution
>   he will come to save you' (NIV).

Similar to the NAB, I do not use quotation marks and leave the extent of the exhortation open. It can be only the first two—Be strong! Do not fear!—with the remainder of v. 4 then addressed to those who are encouraged to strengthen, firm up and speak (vv. 3a-4a).

As already commented on in regard to 34.16, these imperatives with unspecified speaker(s) and addressees continue to stress the openness and expansiveness of the poem. They are addressed to the nations, including Edom, Israel and Babylon, to the creatures of 34.11-15 and to us readers, both ancient and modern. And, in addition, they add a strong element of immediacy: the seeing, the exhortation and the divine appearance are all right now! Finally, whoever the speaker(s) and spoken to, the former mark a bond, a kinship, with the latter, since 'our God' becomes 'your God' with 'your' being masculine plural. From the close of v. 2 through v. 4, 'they', 'we' and 'you' form a varied set of relations with the possibility that 'they' and 'you' may be the same or different. Whether we consider v. 4c—See! Your God!—addressed to the trembling hearted or to those exhorted in 3a-4a adds to the possibilities.

Both 'Strengthen' (חַזְּקוּ; piel imperative) and 'Be strong' (חִזְקוּ; qal imperative) pun on Hezekiah—חִזְקִיָּהוּ, 'may YHWH strengthen' or 'strength of YHWH'—a main character in Isaiah 36–39, first named in 36.1, the first verse immediately after our poem.[105] I note the ambiguous portrait of Hezekiah, the strong and trusting king who is rescued from a military attack (chs. 36–37), the ill man who gets a limited reprieve (ch. 38) and the king who opens all of his palace to the Babylonians (ch. 39). 'To save' (ישׁע) alludes to Isaiah, ישׁעיהו: 'may YHWH save' or 'salvation of YHWH', another main character in chs. 36–39 and the prophet-poet whose vision is recounted in the entire book.[106]

---

105. See 8.11, 22.21 and 41.6-7 for similar puns on Hezekiah commented on in Miscall 1993: 39, 62 and 102. The narratives in Isa. 36–39 are enclosed by the name Hezekiah that occurs in the first and last verses (36.1; 39.8).

106. See Miscall 1993: 36-37 and 107 for further examples and for comment.

'Fear not!' is a formula of assurance that, first, can be addressed by YHWH, or his messenger, to a human whom he appears to, for example, Abram in Gen. 15.1, Jacob in Gen. 26.24 and 46.3 and Gideon in Judg. 6.23, or, secondly, by a human to another human at a time of perceived threat, for example, Joseph to his brothers in Gen. 43.23 and 50.19-21, David to Abiathar in 1 Sam. 22.23 and Jonathan to David in 1 Sam. 23.17. Thirdly, it can be used to encourage a leader or the army at a time of battle or at the threat of attack, for example, YHWH to Moses in Num. 21.34 and Deut. 3.2, Moses to the people in Exod. 14.13, 20.20, Deut. 1.21 and 20.1 and YHWH to Joshua in Josh. 8.1, 10.8 and 11.6. In Isaiah it is spoken by YHWH and the prophet to Ahaz (7.4), the people (10.24) and Hezekiah (37.6)[107] in a war situation and to Jerusalem (40.9), Jacob (41.10, 13-14) and a barren woman (54.4, 14) in a situation of general distress.[108]

Before proceeding with the close reading of this section of the poem, I digress to discuss the continued traces of the early stages of Israel's story. Chapter 35 is reminiscent of exodus–wilderness–conquest because it represents movement through the wilderness into the land, symbolized by Zion. This returns us to the approximate middle of the first part of our poem, 34.9 onwards, and its allusions to the division of the land, dwelling in the land and the ill-fated episode of the monarchy. In ch. 35 the desert is transformed and a road passes through it to Zion. The naming of Zion in 34.8 and in 35.10 frame this entire section of the poem and its latent stories of Israel.

As just noted, יֵשַׁע alludes to Isaiah, יְשַׁעְיְהוּ, but it therefore also alludes to Joshua whose name is the same as Isaiah, 'may YHWH save' or 'salvation of YHWH', except that the theophoric element occurs at the start, not the end, of the name: יְהוֹשֻׁעַ. Joshua is told to be strong (חזק) and firm (אמץ) by Moses (Deut. 31.7), YHWH (Deut. 31.23; Josh 1.6-7) and the people themselves (Josh 1.18). Moses (Deut. 31.8) and YHWH (Josh 1.9) exhort him not to fear. Joshua is assured that YHWH will not fail (רפה) him; this is the root for *weak* hands' in 35.3. (See

This play on the names Hezekiah and Isaiah is part of the prevalent motif of names and naming in Isaiah that I referred to in my discussion of the names in 34.12 (see above, pp. 78-79).

107. Hezekiah, the 'strength of YHWH', is told 'Fear not...for I [YHWH] will have him [Sennacherib] fall by the sword in his land'; this is reminiscent of the effect of YHWH's sword in 34.5-7.

108. See Conrad 1991: 36-49 and Miscall 1993: 125-27 for further discussion of this formula in Isaiah.

David's 'weak hands', or 'discouraged' in the NRSV, in 2 Sam. 17.2.) Faced with the daunting task of conquering the land, Joshua could well be weak-handed or discouraged; he could have faltering knees and a trembling heart, although these terms do not occur with him.[109]

These same verbs for strengthening and firming, חזק and אמץ, are used in their piel stems, the stems used in v. 3, to refer to hardening the heart—whether YHWH hardens Pharaoh's heart (Exod. 4.21; 9.12; 14.4), Sihon's heart (Deut. 2.30), the Canaanites' hearts (Josh. 11.20), or whether the people harden their own hearts (Deut. 15.7). Even in this positive context in Isaiah 35, the prime terms contain denotations of quite other meanings.

Aiding the weak and infirm is an Isaianic theme that can be applied specifically to all Israel, to the remnant and generally to all helpless humans (11.4; 14.30-32; 42.6-9; 57.15).

> The poor and the needy are seeking water and there is none; their tongue
>   is parched with thirst.
> I YHWH answer them; I the God of Israel do not forsake them.
> I open rivers on the bare hills; fountains in the middle of valleys.
> I turn the wilderness into ponds and the dry land into springs of water
>   (41.17-18).

At this point in the poem we picture the people, who are being exhorted, standing and trembling at the preceding visions of wrath, desolation, sudden restoration and divine manifestation. The latter is double-edged. They should be strong and not fearful because God, 'your God', comes to help and, at the same time, they should not fear this divine approach even though it is for the same type of revenge and retaliation as YHWH's 'day of vengeance' (34.8). 'See! Your God!' employs the same particle (הנה) as 'Yes, my sword' in 34.5 and the vengeance alludes to the frightful aftermath of YHWH's retribution (34.8-15). In this brief encouragement, nightmare and dream, YHWH's sword and YHWH himself, demonic land and blooming desert, wrath and joy, all stand in uneasy relationship with neither side able to assume total dominance in our reading.

---

109. It will take another reading to assess the impact of these intertexts in Deuteronomy and Joshua in light of both the parallels noted and the emphasis on sin and anger (Deut. 31.16-18), writing and reading a scroll (Deut. 31.9-13, 19-30; Josh 1.8) and the theme of the ban, the total annihilation of the enemy (Deut. 20; Josh. 6–7).

35.5-7

5   Then are opened the eyes of the blind
        and the ears of the deaf are opened.[110]
6   Then the lame leap like deer
        and the tongue of the speechless sings.
     Indeed waters break forth in the wilderness
        and streams in the desert.[111]
7   And the burning sand is a swamp,
        and the thirsty ground, springs of water.
     In the pasture of jackals is her resting place;[112]
        [her] grass [turns][113] to reed and rush.[114]

In this presentation and division of the poem the preceding exhortation
ends with 'save you' and the poet now reasserts his own voice to affirm

110. I translate both Hebrew verbs as open because they are synonyms and near
homonyms: תִּפָּקַחְנָה and תִּפָּתַחְנָה. The bicolon shares a chiastic structure with 35.3
and I again mark the enclosure with the use of a full stop.

111. In its poetic structure, 6a-b doesn't follow the chiastic pattern of the forego-
ing and employs a more complex structure: particle—verb : simile : subject (one
noun) :: verb : subject (two nouns: construct + genitive). 6c-d does employ a chiastic structure that encloses the bicolon and prepares for the grammatical shift marked
by the וְהָיָה at the start of the next bicolon: particle + verb—accusative of place
('in') : subject :: subject : accusative of place ('in').

112. This colon is a rendering of the MT as it stands. Other translators and commentators want to remove the suffix 'her' on 'resting place'; 'the suff. is, in fact,
incomprehensible' (Wildberger 1982: 1354). Given the importance of pronouns to
my reading, I maintain the suffix.

Wildberger and others employ a relative clause in their renderings: 'An der
Stätte, wo Schakale lagerten, ist Platz für Rohr und Schilf' (Wildberger 1982:
1352); 'The abode where jackals lurk will be a marsh for the reed and papyrus'
(NAB).

NRSV translates 'The haunt of jackals shall become a swamp, the grass shall
become reeds and rushes', and notes that the first colon is a conjecture and that the
Hebrew reads 'in the haunt of jackals is her resting place' which is close to my
translation. See Wildberger 1982: 1354 and Watts 1987: 7 for further discussion of
the Hebrew term and for other possible emendations and translations.

113. Neither 'her' nor 'turns' are in the Hebrew. I supply 'her' in parallel with
the suffix on 'resting place' and 'turns' to make better sense of the terse Hebrew in
English.

114. This is the usual understanding of חָצִיר, but it can also be a biform for חָצֵר,
court or enclosure. See above, p. 82 n. 75, on 34.13. If we accept the latter, we
would have a close parallel to 'her resting place' and the translation would be
something such as '[her] court is among reed and rush' or '[her] court [turns] to
reed and rush'. In either instance the image would be one of growth and lushness.

the effects of the theophany, the encouragement and the retribution. I take the 'then', אָז, at the start of vv. 5a and 6a as a mark of the change from cause to effect. Like כִּי, אָז can be an emphatic adverb or a conjunction;[115] I try to capture both meanings by using 'then' with a present tense in vv. 5-6 and inverted English word order in v. 5a. This rendering indicates a result that is happening at the same time as the cause.

Both verbs for opening are niphals, which indicate passive or middle voice; as so often in the poem, no one, divine or human, actively opens the eyes and ears. Opening assumes a previous closing.

> Go and say to this people:
> 'Listen carefully but don't understand; look closely but don't know'.
> Deaden this people's heart; stop up their ears; seal their eyes—
> Lest they see with their eyes, hear with their ears, understand with their
>   heart and then repent and be healed (6.9-10).[116]

At one point, the deaf hear the words of a scroll (29.17-19) and the poet speaks to deaf and blind other than Israel (42.18-20).

A brief glimpse of the just rule of a king and princes provides an excellent parallel to our passage, 35.5-7, through its imagery of water amid aridity and of the transformation of those physically and mentally impaired.

> See! a king reigns with righteousness and princes rule with justice.
> Each of them is like a refuge from the wind, a shelter from the storm.
> Like streams of water on dry ground, like the shade of a massive rock in
>   a weary land.
> And the eyes of those who see will not be sealed; the ears of those who
> hear will pay attention; the minds of the thoughtless will gain under-
> standing and knowledge; the tongues of stammerers will speak fluently
> (32.1-4).

Seeing and hearing are what we have been doing and have been called to do. This is both the 'we' within the poem, 'our God', and the 'we', the readers, outside the poem. 'Then' (אָז) is therefore not a simple (chrono)logical marker here since 'we' have already been called to hear, to see and to read. Again I emphasize that in our reading, we— the contemporary readers—are invited into and drawn into the poem

---

115. See Waltke and O'Connor 1990: 513-14; 658; 667-68 for discussion and further examples.

116. See 29.9-12 and above, p. 34.

with its scenes that are both frightening and comforting; we are asked to say 'our God'. In this mode of reading, although a hard, unbreachable wall is not erected between the reader and the text, some distance is maintained since we are invited or drawn into the text; we do not simply enter it or become one with it. In addition, I stress that the entire poem describes scenes that are just as much juxtaposed or layered as arranged in a (chrono)logical sequence. We can read the second part of the poem (ch. 35) as simultaneous with the first part (34.1-15), as events happening together, just as readily as we can read it in the traditional sequence of 'the judgment that precedes salvation'. The poem is both a vision and a story even though the two ways of reading stand in tension.

'Eyes' and 'ears' are part of the body imagery of 'hands', 'knees' and 'heart' of vv. 3-4, and they continue this imagery from the first part of the poem, particularly the 'mouth' and 'hand' of 34.16-17 (see above, p. 88). 'Mouth' is matched by the singing 'tongue' of 35.6b and 'hand' by the implied feet and legs, connected by 'faltering knees', that leap in 35.6a. With this imagery the poet introduces physical agility, a new theme in the poem, and he employs another simile, the final one of the poem. 'Like deer' (כְּאַיָּל) echoes the slaughtered animals of 34.6-7, in particular the rams (אֵילִים).

The songs of the speechless evoke the singing of the wilderness and the desert which are blooming and where waters are soon to flow. 'Indeed' renders כִּי of 6c as an emphatic in parallel with the preceding 'then', אָז, of 5a and 6a without nullifying the possible conjunctive sense. Human transformation and restoration are matched by those of nature. This provides another motive for the joy that suffuses this latter half of the poem and another example of the juxtaposition and overlaying of scenes that can also be understood as sequential.

This transformation is the obverse of that other when humans and a flourishing nature were destroyed and desiccated and then replaced by blood, fire, strange creatures and weeds. Water, explicitly absent to this point in the poem, is, however, present in the water imagery of mountains melting with blood and of wadis flowing with pitch. In this context of water, I translate נחלים with 'streams'; in 34.9a, a context of dust, I rendered it with 'wadis'. 'Breaking forth' (נבקעו) is another niphal without an agent. The action alludes to the snake 'hatching eggs' (34.15; see 59.5), to rocks being split or broken so that water can flow (48.21), to light bursting forth (58.8) and to waters being parted so that

Moses and Israel can cross (63.12).

וֹהִיה at the start of v. 7 acts the same as וֹהִיתה in 34.9 and 13. It both emphasizes the preceding theme of transformation and marks a new stage as we now read of inhabitants and events in the changed desert. The bicolon in 7a-b continues the sharp contrast of dry and wet from the previous bicolon and the echoes of the Exodus.

> 'YHWH has redeemed his servant Jacob'.
> They do not thirst when he leads them through the wastes;
> He makes water flow from the rock for them—
> He split the rock and water gushed out! (48.20-21).

The second bicolon in 7c-d contains the only extended literal reference to the first part of the poem, 34.13c-d; the latter is a description of the demonic pasture. The bicolon in 35.7c-d—'And she is a pasture for jackals, grass for ostriches'—is a summarizing and transitional state-ment marking the shift from the description of the transformed site to that of its inhabitants and their activities in 35.8-10.

The bicolon is difficult to interpret. The root for 'resting place', רבץ, is used in contrasting ways in Isaiah and the image recalls both the peaceful kingdom and the demonic realm.

> The wolf dwells with the lamb and the leopard lies down [רבץ] with the
>   kid, the calf, the lion and the fatling all together.
> A small child leads them.
> The cow and the bear graze while their young lie down [רבץ] together;
>   the lion eats straw like the ox (11.6-7).[117]

> She [Lady Babylon] will never be lived in and she will not be dwelt in
>   for all times;
> No Arab will tent there and shepherds will not rest [רבץ] their flocks
>   there.
> Demons will rest [רבץ] there and howling creatures will fill their houses;
> Ostriches will dwell there and hairy-demons will cavort there (13.20-21;
>   see 17.2).[118]

'She' in 35.7 is yet another pronoun with ambiguous antecedent. Is 'she' Zion, Edom or even Lilith who is still on the scene? With the latter reading, which I strongly maintain as an alternative, the poet gives us a final glimpse of the wild and demonic inhabitants of the desolate wastes before turning to the highway that is there and that is

117. See previous citation on p. 81.
118. 13.19-22 was cited previously; see p. 60.

separate from its environs. Whether we interpret חָצִיר as 'grass' or as a 'court' or 'enclosure', the point is its change and its resultant lushness: it turns to or serves as a place for swamp plants. If we take 'she' as Lilith, we see that her abode is changing for the better although she is still to be excluded from the highway that traverses her land.

35.8-10

8   There emerges there a highway, yes,[119] a way;
        The Holy Way it is called to her.[120]
     The unclean do not pass over it;
        it is for him/them[121] who walk(s) the way;[122]
     fools do not wander [on it].[123]
9   There is not there[124] a lion,
        nor does a ravenous beast[125] go up on it;
     she is not found there.[126]

119. Translating the waw as epexegetical; see Waltke and O'Connor 1990: 648-49, 652-53 and my comments on 34.1 (above pp. 28-29).

120. 'To her' can refer to the way, דֶּרֶךְ, which can be feminine despite the fact that it is referred to with masculine pronouns in the next bicolon. Or 'to her' can refer to the desert, the feminine referent in vv. 1-2. 'It is called to her' can be 'she is named' or 'it is read to her' to reflect the variety of meanings possible for קָרָא.

121. לָמוֹ means both 'to him' and 'to them'.

122. This line division and translation are indebted to Watts's 'It is for the one who walks The Way' (see the NIV). Watts (1987: 7) notes that the *athnah* on לָמוֹ breaks a colon and he accepts the division presented in *BHS*. Note the parallel phrase and concept in 33.15: 'he who walks righteously'. The JPS maintains the break marked by the *athnah* and renders: 'No one unclean shall pass along it, but it shall be for them. No traveler, not even fools, shall go astray'. The translators do note that the Hebrew of the final colon is uncertain.

123. The final phrase is supplied from the sense of the context.

124. 'There is not there', לֹא יִהְיֶה שָׁם, is emphatic in Hebrew because of the use of the *yiqtol* of the connective verb 'is', יִהְיֶה, and because of the contrast with the previous 'there emerges there', וְהָיָה שָׁם, in 8a.

125. For this particular construction in which the adjective appears in the construct state and the noun in the genitive—'ravenous—of beasts'—see GKC 132c.

126. In this instance, I, in agreement with most translations, read with the *athnah* on שָׁם in the MT and don't follow *BHS*'s division that would place שָׁם with גְּאוּלִים וְהָלְכוּ: 'there the redeemed walk'. Wildberger (1982: 1354), 'according to general opinion', regards the phrase לֹא תִמָּצֵא שָׁם as superfluous. He places שָׁם with the last phrase of v. 9 but puts it after וְהָלְכוּ and avoids the problem of dealing with the waw on the verb that arises if we follow the actual MT text: שָׁם וְהָלְכוּ גְּאוּלִים. I take the waw as disjunctive and render 'but'.

9d   But they walk,[127] the redeemed,
10   yes, the ransomed of YHWH, they return;
      They come to Zion[128] with song,
          yes, everlasting joy on their heads.
      Rejoicing and joy, they attain[129]
          and they flee, grief and sighing.

I render וְהָיָה 'there emerges', rather than 'there is', to capture the sense that the following scene shifts the focus and is only loosely connected with the preceding. The impersonal sense of 'there emerges' fits with the passive or middle sense of much of the poem. 'There', שָׁם, occurs three times in these lines matching the threefold emphasis in 34.14-15. The scene in these final verses is set in the wilderness, whether we envision the latter as demonic, transformed or a mixture of the two. The highway suddenly appears in this wilderness or it is already there and just now brought into sight. The remainder of the poem, then, describes who and what are not on and are on this highway, echoing the description of the demonic realm at the close of the first part of the poem.

מַסְלוּל, highway, is a *hapax* in the Hebrew Bible and perhaps an Isaianic neologism formed to contrast with מְסִלָּה, the usual term in Isaiah and the Hebrew Bible for highway (Isa. 7.3; 36.2; 40.3; 59.7). The unusual term is explicated by the ordinary term דֶּרֶךְ, way or road,

Even with תִמָּצֵא, third person feminine singular, he maintains that יִמָּצֵא, third person masculine singular, would be the expected form: '[man trifft es nicht]'. Other translations simply gloss over the impact of the third person feminine singular form by translating with a masculine or neutral form. 'They [beasts] shall not be found there' (NRSV; see JPS and NIV); 'not one [savage beast] will be found there' (REB); and 'nothing of the sort be found' (NJB). I keep the third person feminine form because of the frequency of the feminine singular in other parts of the poem. Finally, 'she is not found there' is stressed because it stands separate from the preceding two cola of the tricolon. 9a-b is enclosed in a chiastic structure: verb : subject :: subject : verb.

127. I do not supply a 'there' from the context since this would turn the focus on the highway and not on the goal, Zion, or on the movement itself.

128. בּוֹא is usually followed by a preposition or -*āh* directive to mark the destination of the movement but this is not always the case; see Judg. 20.26; 21.2; Jer. 20.6; 34.3; 44.12 and Amos 4.4 for exceptions. Isa. 52.8 contains the same construction with שׁוּב in a passage that forms an interesting parallel to that in our poem. 'Plainly they see YHWH's return to Zion'.

129. The line can be translated as 'they attain/reach rejoicing and joy' (see NRSV and JPS). See Watts 1987: 7 and Wildberger 1982: 1355 for discussion including 1QIsaᵃ.

that is marked as epexegetical by the waw (Waltke and O'Connor 1990: 648-49, 652-53). I regard the explication ודרך as an integral part of the text and not as a later editorial or scribal gloss even though the term is omitted by 1QIsaᵃ. I reiterate that I treat text-critical issues more as matters of alternative readings than as matters of the true text, the Urtext.

Both highway and road have a mix of the literal and the figurative, that is, the physical road and the proper moral, religious way. The same multi-levelled meaning is found elsewhere in Isaiah (48.15-17; 55.7-8). The nations want to ascend the mountain of YHWH's house so 'that he may teach us his ways and that we may walk in his paths' (2.3). 'For thus YHWH said to me as he took my hand; he warned me not to walk in this people's way' (8.11). The following passage shares several parallels with our poem.

> In the wilderness prepare the way of YHWH,
> make straight in the desert a highway for our God.
> Let every valley be lifted up, and every mountain and hill made low;
> and the uneven ground will become level, and the rough places a plain
> (40.3).

To be holy is to be set aside, to be dedicated to a special purpose or status, particularly a divine one. God is holy and association with him makes a person, an act or a thing holy. The highway is holy because it is set aside, different from its environs, and because it is dedicated to YHWH's ransomed. In Isaiah YHWH is the Holy One of Israel (1.4; 17.7; 31.1; 41.16; 55.5; 60.14). He has his holy mountain (11.9; 56.7; 66.20), his holy arm (52.10), day (58.13) and spirit (63.10-11). Zion is the holy city (48.2; 52.1) and Israel the holy people (63.18). 'I am YHWH your God, the Holy One of Israel, your Savior' (43.3) and 'YHWH, your Redeemer, the Holy One of Israel' (43.14). These passages and the following all connect holiness, salvation and redemption in ways similar to those in our poem.

> Tell daughter Zion, 'See, your salvation comes;
> See, his reward is with him and his recompense before him'.
> They call them, 'The Holy People, The Redeemed of YHWH'.
> And you [Zion] are called, 'Sought Out, A City Not Forsaken' (62.11-
> 12).

In the closing verses of ch. 35 the poet first tells us what humans and animals are not there on the holy way and then who is there and what they are doing. The unclean, טמא, is a general category that includes both humans and animals. It reflects the purity system of priestly material, for example, Leviticus, Numbers and Ezekiel and usually stands in contrast with the clean (טהור).[130] In a certain sense, to be unclean is the opposite of being holy since the unclean should have no association with God or with anything holy. 'Holy, Holy, Holy! YHWH, God of Hosts!' (6.3; see 57.15). Faced with this presence of the Holy One, Isaiah reacts by thinking that he is doomed because he is a man of 'unclean lips' dwelling in 'the midst of a people of unclean lips' (6.5).[131]

In Isaiah the verb 'to be clean' occurs in parallel with the verb 'to be holy' in a sarcastic comment on sinners who eat the unclean flesh of pigs (see Lev. 11.7-8 and Deut. 14.8). 'Those who sanctify themselves and cleanse themselves for the gardens…eating pigs' flesh…will perish together' (66.17). The only other occurrence of 'clean' is at the end of the book and shares the theme of movement towards Zion-Jerusalem with the end of our poem.

> They bring all your kin from all the nations as an offering to YHWH…on my holy mountain Jerusalem, says YHWH, just as the Israelites bring the offering, in a clean vessel, to the house of YHWH (66.20).

The 'unclean' is in parallel with 'fools', אוילים, a wisdom term that is frequent in Proverbs (10.8, 10; 14.3, 9; 20.3; 27.3, 22).

> The fear of YHWH is the essence of knowledge;
> Fools despise wisdom and discipline (Prov. 1.7).

The only other occurrence of the term in Isaiah is in the denunciation of Egypt's princes as 'total fools' (19.11). Wisdom, especially as expressed in the book of Proverbs, stands at the other end of the religious spectrum from priestly purity represented by 'unclean/clean'. Thus the tricolon in 8c-e, in a merismus of 'priest and wise man', encompasses the religious value system of the Hebrew Bible. This is similar to the phrase 'priest and prophet reel with strong drink' in 28.7. In the center of the tricolon are those 'who walk the way' without reference to any specific religious or moral system.

---

130. In v. 8a for ודרך LXX reads ὁδὸς χαθαρά, 'the clean way', probably טהור or ברור (see *BHS* notes), a clear contrast to טמא.

131. Neither the uncircumcised nor the unclean can enter the holy city (52.1) and the people are to touch nothing unclean as they leave Babylon (52.11). The people confess that they are like something unclean (64.5).

> The unclean do not pass over it;
> > it is for those who walk the way;
> Fools do not wander on it.

Pass over and wander, even though grammatically negative, connote movement and the theme is emphasized in the central colon: he who walks the way. The movement of this closing scene balances the movement of the descent of wrath, sword and victims and of the ascent of stench and smoke which characterize the opening scenes in 34.1-10. 'Pass over' is the same verb, עבר, rendered 'pass through' in 34.10 in the assertion that none pass through the desolate and smoldering land. This use of the same verb, although with different subjects, makes an interesting connection between the demonic land and the holy way, a connection related to our distinction of manifest and latent meanings and to the way that these meanings can switch places. In ch. 34 the demonic is the manifest and the holy the latent meaning and vice versa in ch. 35.

In 35.8 the manifest meaning is that the unclean and fools are nowhere on the highway. However, there is a latent meaning, a play on the double meaning of the Hebrew verbs, in which even the unclean and fools are part of the transformation to the better. Both עבר and תעה, besides denoting actual physical movement also mean, respectively, to pass beyond in the sense of to transgress, to violate, and to wander away from the right, to err.

> The earth lies polluted beneath its inhabitants for they have violated (עבר) laws, they have broken statutes, they have destroyed the eternal covenant (24.5).

> My people, those who should direct you mislead (תעה) you (3.12).[132]

Thus the first and last cola of the tricolon in 35.8c-e connote not transgressing or erring and can be rendered 'The unclean do not transgress it...Fools do not err'. This is particularly so with the final colon that doesn't have a term or pronoun for 'there' or 'way'.

The next tricolon, v. 9, shifts to describe the animals who are not there: lions, ravenous beasts and 'she'. I take 'she' to be Lilith who is in the surrounding wilderness, resting in the jackals' pasture, but who does not venture on to the highway. The beasts not going up is another

132. See 9.15 and 19.13-14. For further examples of this use of עבר, see Num. 14.41, Judg. 2.20, 1 Sam. 15.24, 2 Kgs 18.12 and Prov. 8.29. For תעה, see Isa. 28.7, 29.24, 63.17, Ezek. 14.11, Ps. 58.4 and Prov. 7.25 and 14.22.

allusion to the stench and the smoke that do go up (34.3, 10). Before depicting the highway itself in the last three bicola, the poet gives us a final overview of the surrounding desert and its inhabitants and continues the mixing and mingling of dream and nightmare, of the demonic realm and the peaceable kingdom. Whether this surrounding wilderness is the demonic realm of the first part of the poem or the transformed desert of this part remains an open question and this contributes to the mixing.

'But', which introduces the first of the final three bicola and, in a sense, all three bicola, highlights the contrast between those who aren't on the highway and those who are. I translate 9d-10a with broken word order to reflect the structure of the bicolon which is framed in a chiastic structure by the verbs of motion which are general, 'walk', and goal-oriented, 'return'; the noun and noun phrase, then, stand in the center in an explicative or emphatic relationship.

> But they walk,
> The redeemed, yes, the ransomed of YHWH,
> They return.

At the close of ch. 1, Zion herself is ransomed through justice and those who return to her, or those in her who repent, through righteousness (1.27).[133] 'The redeemer comes to Zion, to Jacob, to those who turn from rebellion' (59.20). שוב, to turn and return, has, at different points in Isaiah, both meanings of physical return and moral return or repentance.[134] Thus the people on the holy way in our poem are returning both to Zion and to YHWH's paths and ways.

Ransom, פדה, is not a frequent term in Isaiah. Other than the use in 1.27 and the repetition of 35.10 in 51.11, the term occurs twice and asserts YHWH's redemptive power. 'YHWH is the one who ransomed Abraham' (29.22). 'Is my hand too short to ransom?' (50.2). Redeem, גאל, and the participle 'redeemer', are frequent and, with the exception

---

133. 'Justice' is משפט which occurs in 34.5; see my previous discussion on pp. 49-50 for comments on the pair 'justice and righteousness'.

134. The physical sense is in the return of Sennacherib (37.7-8), the sundial (38.8) and YHWH (52.8). The moral sense of return, repentance, is found in 6.10, 19.22, 44.22 and 55.7. Both senses are contained in the name of Isaiah's son Shear-jashub, 'a remnant will return', since the return is to the actual land and to the ways of YHWH (7.3; 10.21-22). The two senses are in 55.10-11 in the extended comparison between the descent of rain and snow and of YHWH's word; none of them returns without accomplishing its purpose.

of this poem, their occurrences are all in the latter half of the book.
Most of the occurrences are in divine titles such as 'Your Redeemer,
the Holy One of Israel' (41.14; 43.14)[135] and 'Our Redeemer, YHWH of
hosts is his name' (47.4; see 44.6).[136] The verb occurs in assertions of
YHWH's redemption of his people. 'O Israel! Do not fear for I have
redeemed you' (43.1). 'Return to me for I have redeemed you (44.22).
The latter combines 'redeem' with the moral sense of return. 'YHWH
has redeemed Jacob and is glorified in Israel' (44.23). In 49.26 and
60.16, the poet combines redeem and save in a divine declaration to
Zion: 'I am YHWH, your Savior and your Redeemer, the Bull of
Jacob'.[137]

In contrast to the majority of these occurrences that portray YHWH as
the active redeemer, our passage employs an indirect passive, 'the
redeemed, yes, the ransomed of YHWH'.[138] Characteristic of our poem,
the poet does not state explicitly that YHWH has redeemed these people
and he does not further identify them. The large majority, if not all, of
the other references to redeem and ransom in Isaiah would lead us to
assume that these are the Israelites returning to Zion from their exile
and following the horrific judgment on the nations in the first half of the
poem. This is certainly the understanding of most, if not all, commentaries on the poem. However, as noted consistently throughout our
reading, the poem itself does not support such a focused and unam-
biguous identification of those returning or of any of the other groups in
the poem. I repeat that this is not a poem that clearly contrasts doomed
nations with saved Israel. Those returning, the redeemed, can be
Israelites or any among the nations, or even among the inhabitants of
the desolate land, who joyfully have turned to see 'the splendor of our
God'.

As an added departure from the usual reading of the poem, we can
regard YHWH's redeemed as yet another group, related to but different
from those earlier in the poem who are rejoicing, those who see the
glory of YHWH, those who encourage and those who are encouraged to

135. The same phrase occurs in 48.17 and 54.5; a closely related form is in 49.7.
136. See 44.24, 49.26 (= 60.16), 54.8, 59.20 and 63.16 for other titles.
137. Redeem and save are associated in context in 49.6-7, 52.9-10, 62.11-12 and
63.8-9. 62.11-12, cited above on p. 109, combines themes of salvation, holiness and
redemption.
138. The past participles occur elsewhere in Isaiah only in 51.10 and 62.12
(גאולים) and in 51.11 (פדויים).

help the blind and weak. The transformation of the wilderness occurs, the highway appears in its midst and the redeemed of YHWH abruptly appear on it moving towards Zion. This accords with the poet's consistent use of pronouns and adverbs, his limited use of proper names and his refusal to identify and delineate definitively all of the characters and places involved.

Song and joy close out the last half of our poem and form an inclusion with the joy and shouts of the desert that open it. On the other hand, the theme of sound and noise looks back to the call to hear and to pay attention that opens the entire poem. Everlasting joy, שמחת עולם, contrasts with the everlasting smoke and desolation of the demonic land (34.10); everlasting possession is affirmed in the middle of these contrasting states (34.17).

Even though the bicolon 9d-10a is closed in its structure, it introduces the succession of three verbs ending in the arrival at Zion: they walk (הלך), they return (שוב), they come (בוא).[139] The arrival at the goal is formally marked by the enjambment of 10c—'They come to Zion with song, yes, everlasting joy on their heads'—that contrasts with the chiastic structure of both 9d-10a and 10d-e. I translate the middle 'with song, yes, everlasting joy' with the same explicative, emphatic relationship as in the preceding bicolon.

The movement on the road, the ability to walk, refer back to the strengthening of knees and the agility of the lame; 'their heads' refer, through body imagery, to the opened eyes and ears and to the tongue that can now sing (see above, p. 88).[140] Their goal Zion, ציון, forms an added inclusion through the pun on 'dry land', ציה, in 35.1 which itself is rejoicing because of this highway and its travellers. Both Zion and dry land allude to the 'phantoms', ציים, that inhabit the demonic realm (34.14a).

Zion is the goal of the redeemed, those who follow the way and those who walk on the holy road. Zion, with her frequent parallel Jerusalem, is the holy city, עיר הקדש (48.2; 52.1), that the holy way, דרך הקדש, leads to. Zion-Jerusalem is YHWH's holy mountain (2.2-3; 24.23) where he dwells (8.18; 18.7; 31.9) and is often called Mount Zion (4.5; 10.12, 32). She was established by YHWH (14.32; 28.16) and filled with

139. The verbs themselves form a chiastic structure according to their form: *weqatal—yiqtol—weqatal*. In Hebrew 'they return and they come' are separated only by a line break, not by other words: ישבון ובאו.

140. The root רנן occurs in both 6b and 10b and in 2b.

'justice and righteousness' (33.5; see 1.27).[141] Besides being the city, whether actual or glorified, Zion-Jerusalem is also a personified charac- ter, a woman, who speaks and is spoken to.

> Shout aloud and sing for joy, O reigning Zion,[142]
> for great in your midst is the Holy One of Israel (12.6).

> She despises you [king of Assyria], she mocks you, Maiden Daughter Zion!
> Behind you she tosses her head, Daughter Jerusalem! (37.22).

> But Zion says, 'YHWH has forsaken me, my lord has forgotten me'.
> Does a woman forget her infant showing no compassion for the child of her womb?
> Even if these could forget, I, I will not forget you (49.14-15).

In a passage that shares both the imagery and particular terminology of a transformed waste, the poet asserts YHWH's care for the city.

> YHWH indeed comforts Zion, he comforts all her wastes;[143]
> He makes her wilderness like Eden, her desert like the garden of YHWH.
> Rejoicing and joy are found in her, thanksgiving songs and the sound of music (51.3).

Rejoicing and joy, שׂשׂון ושׂמחה, are the same pair that occur in 35.10d. In both passages, 35.10 and 51.3, rejoicing and joy are associated with Zion.

However, in our poem, both here and in 34.8, only Zion is named and she is simply named; it is not clear whether we are to think of Zion as the city or as the glorified city, 'the city of YHWH' (60.14). Jerusalem is not mentioned despite the fact that the city is the focus of

141. See Webb 1990 for a brief but insightful overview of the role of Zion in Isaiah.

142. Many translations take the feminine participle יושׁבת as referring to those dwelling in Zion and not as an attribute of Zion. Watts (1985: 181-82) renders 'inhabitant of Zion' and notes 'Fem. to indicate a collective sense'. Others are similar, although many use the plural: 'You who dwell in Zion' (JPS); 'People of Zion' (NIV) and 'You dwellers in Zion' (REB). However, in Isaiah, Zion—whether the city or a woman personified—is referred to using feminine singular forms and therefore, in this passage, I translate the participle as referring directly to Zion. This is similar to NRSV, 'O royal Zion', although there is a translator's note on 'royal': 'Or *O inhabitant of*'.

143. This is the plural of חָרְבָּה that was discussed in relation to the desolate land in 34.10 (see above, pp. 71-72). Both noun and verb share the root חרב.

the narratives in Isaiah 36–39 and is first named in 36.2. Immediately before the start of our poem, she is paired with Zion in 33.20.

> Envision Zion, our festive city! Your eyes see Jerusalem:
> A quiet homestead, a tent not to be moved.

This lack of specificity is the same as with 'the ransomed of YHWH'. Despite the fact that the majority of the book of Isaiah would lead us to assume a lot about the exact identity and characteristics of the ransomed and of Zion in this poem, our poet maintains his distinctive reticence and ambiguity even when using titles and names such as the ransomed and Zion. There is joy and transformation; waters flow and people walk; the redeemed return to Zion. This vision, this dream, stands juxtaposed with the scenes of the nightmare land when YHWH's vengeance falls on his doomed people and he enacts retribution 'for Zion's case'. All of it is contained in the scroll of YHWH.

The bicolon of 9d-10a is enclosed in its chiastic structure and yet continued in the enjambment of 10b-c. In the final bicolon of 10d-e, however, the poet reverses the verb–noun structure of 9d-10a that placed the nouns in the center and produces a neat parallelism that places the verbs in the middle—noun : noun : verb :: verb : noun : noun. On the other hand, the content of the two bicola comprises the sharp contrast of attaining and fleeing and of joy and grief. Happiness approaches while misery flees. The contrasting movements form a fitting close to a poem that begins with the approach of the nations to hear of wrath and rage.

It is difficult to reflect fully the ambiguity of 10d in English translation. שָׂשׂוֹן וְשִׂמְחָה יַשִּׂיגוּ: the two nouns can be both subject and object. Rejoicing and joy attain or reach out to Zion and to the redeemed returning to her and, at the same time, they are attained, experienced, by the latter when they arrive at Zion. In 10e grief and sighing are the subject since 'flee', וְנָסוּ, would require a preposition 'from', such as מִן, if the redeemed were the subject. Further this is a joyous arrival. Misery flees. Depicting the ransomed fleeing would introduce a too negative note into this closing scene. And yet, true to the ambiguity of the poem and its layering of manifest and latent content in the unresolved contrast of nightmare and dream, the poem closes with this juxtaposition of happiness and misery and of success and flight. Even if they are said to

flee, the last two words of the poem are 'grief and sighing, יגון ואנחה'.[144]
They contrast sharply with the joy and song that open the last part of
our poem in 35.1-2 and accord with the fury and violence that open the
whole poem in 34.1-4.

144. The tightness of the final bicolon is marked at the phonic level. Of the 27
characters that comprise the bicolon in the MT, 5 are sibilants, שׁ and ס, and
4 nasals, מ and נ. Both sets of nouns have end-rhyme. The first two end with the
syllable *-ôn*, וֹן-, and the final two with *-ḥâ*, חָה-. Both verbs have sibilants and end
with the vowel *û*, ו.

Chapter 3

READING ISAIAH

The Vision

In this final section, I discuss the poem's setting in Isaiah and the implications of the analysis of the poem and of the overall mode of reading for a continued reading and appreciation of Isaiah's vision. To a large extent this will be a summary and development of many points and comments already made that are relevant to these topics. I have consistently referred to and, at many points, cited material from throughout Isaiah for a variety of reasons. For the immediate context I have noted parallels with chs. 32–33 and 36–39; I have quoted frequently and usually at length from chs. 32–33 but only occasionally and briefly from 36–39. The poem shares much in terms of terminology, themes and imagery with all of Isaiah and with its immediate context in the book; as stated in the Introduction, it is an integral part of Isaiah's vision. On the other hand, again as noted in the Introduction (see above, pp. 17-18), Isaiah 34–35 is a separate poem because of its details, structure and length. The distinctiveness is just as much, if not more, a matter of form, how it says it, as a matter of content, what it says.

The first obvious implication for study of the entire vision of Isaiah is the extension of this mode of open and expansive close reading to other parts of the book and to all of Isaiah to explore the results of such readings of Isaiah and to compare and contrast them with this reading of Isaiah 34–35. The poem is an integral, yet distinct, part of the book and I have supported this with general and specific material from Isaiah, ranging from large-scale patterns and imagery to the use of individual roots and words. Yet, pending similar readings of a significant amount of Isaiah, I am not able to expand the assertion to wider, more specific and inclusive statements of just how the poem does and does not fit with Isaiah.

For example, in this reading I have stressed the poet's relegation of YHWH to the background; he is not the active character that he is in other parts of Isaiah. The poet's focus is on the effects and not on the actor(s) or actions that produce them. I have also emphasized that the poet, although detailed in the descriptions of both nightmare and dream scenes, does not finally identify or name the locations beyond the generic terms land and wilderness. Edom and its capital Bozrah may be the site of the nightmare land or they may be only the starting-point for the spreading effects of the divine sword; the descriptions in ch. 34 allude to Zion and her land Israel, Sodom and Gomorrah, and Babylon.

This treatment of YHWH and the locations forms a contrast with the immediate context, particularly chs. 36–39, where YHWH is an actor and Zion-Jerusalem a focus of the activity.

> Envision Zion, our festive city! Your eyes see Jerusalem...
> For YHWH is our judge, YHWH is our lawgiver, YHWH is our king,
>   YHWH saves us (33.20-22).[1]

> From Jerusalem a remnant will go forth and a group of survivors from Mount Zion. The zeal of YHWH of hosts is doing this. Therefore thus says YHWH to the king of Assyria: 'He will not enter this city...I will defend this city to save it for my sake and for the sake of David my servant' (37.32-35).

However, even this limited assertion is qualified by the phrase 'particularly in chs. 36–39' since neither YHWH nor Zion-Jerusalem play the same central roles in the immediately preceding chapters as they do in chs. 36–37. For example, neither is mentioned in ch. 32 (see above, p. 104, for a citation of the first four verses). In 32.9-20 the poet begins by denouncing the complacent women and then shifts to describing the transformation of the wilderness (see above, pp. 82-83, for vv. 14-18); the transition is marked by a declaration that is reminiscent of our poem because of its passive voice, its use of 'spirit' and not YHWH himself and the ambiguous 'us'. In 34.16-17 YHWH's mouth, breath and hand are the actors and not YHWH himself (see above, p. 88); 'breath' is the same term, רוּחַ, translated 'spirit' in 32.15.

> Both hill and tower are now dens forever, the joy of asses, pasture for flocks
> Until *a spirit is poured out on us* from on high
> And the wilderness becomes farm land and farm land is thought of as a forest (32.14-15).

1. See above, p. 73.

YHWH is active in ch. 31 and Zion-Jerusalem is the immediate recipient of his interventions.

> So will YHWH of hosts descend to fight upon Mount Zion and upon its hill.
> Like hovering birds will YHWH of hosts shield Jerusalem: shielding and delivering, sparing and rescuing...says YHWH: his fire is in Zion and his furnace in Jerusalem (31.4-5, 9).

This example illustrates the need for a thorough and close reading of the rest of Isaiah before general and limited assertions of how our poem fits and doesn't fit can be extended to more specific and inclusive claims. This particular instance would lead to in-depth studies of how YHWH is presented in the vision, with close attention to changes in that presentation as we move through the changing scenes and speeches of the book; the studies would not be conducted on the assumption that YHWH is always presented the same throughout the vision. Following are some of the questions that could guide such studies, but they are not asked on the assumption that they can always be answered or that they can be answered with one, clear, univocal answer. What titles and names are applied to YHWH? In what contexts? When is he present and when isn't he even mentioned? Is he an active or passive character? Is he at the center of the scene or relegated to the background? Is he an actor and/or speaker? What does he do or say and to whom? Why does he act or speak? Similar readings would also trace the changing presentation of Zion-Jerusalem throughout the vision. I discussed this in part previously in connection with Zion's appearance in 34.8 (see above, pp. 57-61) and 35.10 (see above, pp. 114-16).

These particular studies, among others, would be conducted within the framework of this mode of open, expansive reading and with full respect for the differences that are found throughout Isaiah's vision, especially those of form and style. Throughout this study of Isaiah 34–35, our reading has been concerned with how the poet says and presents the scenes just as much as, if not more than, with what he says. This concern entails close attention to poetic style that includes figurative language, parallelism (syntactic, semantic, grammatical and phonetic), imagery, word-play, assonance, and so on. Isaiah's poetry, in part, accomplishes its effects, its impact, through an impressionistic style that juxtaposes or piles up images, scenes, speeches, and so on. It works within the tension of vision and narrative, of envisioning all of Isaiah now and of seeing Isaiah, or parts of Isaiah such as the scenes in our poem, in a (chrono)logical development.

Concern for diversity in Isaiah, whether in form or content, should always stand in tension or balance with an awareness of the regularity found in Isaiah, the repetition and development of terminology, images, themes and styles. Further, this mode of reading is open to plurality, ambiguity and undecidability since not all questions asked of the text can be answered or answered with only one, certain answer. For example, not all pronouns have identifiable antecedents. We may often have to describe groups or individuals, for example, 'we', 'you' and 'he', and the relations between them, without being able to identify them by name, by matching them with others named in the vision. It is reading that can hover between alternative interpretations without having to choose one or the other. For example, moving beyond our poem, the close of Isaiah 47 describes Lady Babylon and/or Zion-Jerusalem ('you' is feminine singular; see above, pp. 60-61):

> But now hear this, O voluptuous woman, you who reign securely,
> You who say in your heart, 'I am and there is none other but me.
> I do not reign as a widow; I do not experience the loss of children'.
> Both of these will happen to you in a moment, in one day:
> The loss of children and widowhood will happen to you in full measure
> Despite your many enchantments and the great power of your spells.
> You trust in your evil; you say, 'No one sees me'.
> Your wisdom and your skill, they lead you astray,
> And you say in your heart, 'I am and there is none other but me'.
> But evil happens to you which you cannot conjure away;
> Disaster falls upon you which you are unable to avert;
> Ruin happens to you suddenly and you had no hint of it.
> Stand firm in your spells and in your many enchantments,
> Which you have practiced to exhaustion from your youth;
> Perhaps you'll be able to succeed; perhaps you'll strike terror—
> You are worn out with your many consultations.
> Let them stand and save you, those who study the heavens and gaze at
>   the stars,
> Those who predict at each new moon what will happen to you.
> But look, they are like stubble, fire burns them;
> They cannot save themselves from the power of the flame.
> This is not a coal to warm oneself by nor a fire to sit before!
> Such to you are they with whom you have exhaustively traded from your
>   youth—
> Each wanders on his own way—there is none to save you! (47.8-15).

It is a fantastic way of reading that focuses on the manifest text and meaning and yet, at the same time, respects latent texts and meanings that may contrast with and unsettle our reading of the manifest text. This is slightly different than maintaining two or more possible interpretations of a text since the latent meaning(s) does not have to have the status of an alternative interpretation. I have tried to capture this quality with phrases such as 'shadow reading' and 'elusive allusions'. Examples are the allusions in ch. 34 to better times, to more favorable meanings of words and phrases and to a more active and beneficent YHWH. The manifest nightmare is unsettled by traces of dreams. In analyzing ch. 34 I noted, at several points, the shadow reading of Israel's own story from the conquest and division of the land under Joshua's leadership, including both hopes for a perfect life in the land and the troubled history and eventual downfall of the monarchy. The latter, however, serves to confirm the nightmare; the latent dream itself contains a grim story.

Such doubled reading, maintaining both nightmare and dream, both horror and fairy-tale fantasy, is a main characteristic of my reading. Our poem, in its descriptions of both grim and marvelous transformations and scenes, holds the tension between times of misery such as oppression in Egypt, wandering in the wilderness and exile in Babylon and times of hope and prosperity such as Exodus, divine guidance and sustenance in the wilderness, entrance into the land and return from exile. If we read the poem in a strict (chrono)logical, narrative frame, then we can say that all the times of misery and places of suffering are left behind as the redeemed of YHWH return to Zion. Yet even this strict reading is unsettled, to some extent, by the last two words of the poem, 'grief and sighing'; even if they are portrayed as fleeing the scene in Zion, they are still present in the text.

On the other hand, we can, at the same time, read in an atemporal, visionary frame in which we keep all the times and scenes of the poem present in our reading and in our imagination. Hard times and good times, desolation and renewal, judgment and salvation all exist at once and together. I want to explore this latter point a little further because I think that it is a central part of a poetic, visionary reading of Isaiah and this centrality is indicated, in part, by the presence of our poem in the very middle of the book and vision of Isaiah. And I want to connect it with the similar feature in which the status and the fates of Israel and the nations are both sharply contrasted and inextricably intertwined; this has been discussed in the Introduction and in the course of the reading (see above, pp. 15-17 and 95-98). The confusion of Babylon and Zion at the close of Isaiah 47 is a striking example of this intertwining, this overlapping, of opposites.

To reiterate the previous points, the inclusive, encyclopedic aspects of Isaiah comprise this panorama of humanity. In one frame Israel is YHWH's chosen people who stand in strong opposition to the rest of the nations, particularly the powerful empires of Assyria and Babylon. In another frame Israel stands with other nations as a peer, as part of YHWH's people who are all humanity. In yet another frame Israel melds into humanity and all are either devastated or saved by YHWH. These frames alternate throughout the book; no one frame is confined to or dominates a particular part of the book. Isaiah is not a simple tale in which Israel gradually separates himself from the other nations or in which Israel begins as separate and then merges with the nations to form all humanity by the close of the book. Israel, the nations and humanity are all present at the beginning and at the end of Isaiah and throughout the rest of Isaiah's vision.

This juxtaposition and intermixing of the different groups of humanity is accompanied by a similar presentation of scenes of peace and war and of prosperity and desolation. Fantasies and nightmares alternate and intermingle. Salvation and judgment go hand in hand and are not always presented in a strict chronological succession in which the former follows and is clearly distinguished from the latter. Finally, this mixing includes the evaluation of different groups or parts of groups as good or evil or as righteous or wicked and as therefore deserving of reward or punishment. But these are not hard-and-fast distinctions in Isaiah's vision.

> I am YHWH and there is no other. I form light and I create darkness. I make peace and I create evil.[2] I YHWH make all these things (45.6-7).

Isaiah's vision is not a simple morality play in which the good prosper and the wicked suffer. YHWH is with his servants, who can be his people, and against his enemies, who can also be his people (1.24). However, because of the noticeable lack of any explicit mention of righteousness or sin as motivation for either the restoration or the deso-

---

2. This is a shocking statement that is usually softened in translations, except for KJV—'I make peace, and create evil'. NAB, NRSV and TNK contrast 'weal' or 'well-being' and 'woe'; GNB 'blessing' and 'disaster'; NIV 'prosperity' and 'disaster'; and NJB 'well-being' and 'disaster'.

lation of the two parts of our poem, I am not going to develop this issue of moral evaluation beyond my earlier comments (see above, pp. 63-69).

As illustrated at points throughout the reading, much of this intermingling derives from the poet's use of the same or similar images to depict both salvation and judgment and from the fact that whether we are reading and envisioning a dream or a nightmare, hints and shadows of the other linger to upset our attempts to read a given text as only a dream or a nightmare, as only salvation or judgment. For example, water is both 'the waters of Shiloah that flow gently' and 'the mighty and massive waters of the River…[that] rise out of all their channels and go over all their banks' (8.6-7). It is the flood that threatens the over-confident rulers of Jerusalem.[3]

> I make justice the measuring line and righteousness the weight.
> Hail will sweep away the false refuge and waters will flood your shelter.
> Your covenant with Death will be annulled and your pact with Sheol
> will not stand;
> The raging flood will certainly pass through[4] and you will be like
> trampled ground (28.17-18).[5]

Water can be the devastating flood waters of Noah (54.9) or the threatening waters of the deep that YHWH divides for Moses and the Israelites (63.12-13). On the other hand, it can also be an image for the knowledge of YHWH completely filling the earth 'as the waters cover the sea' (11.9) and the sustenance that YHWH provides for the thirsty.

> The poor and the needy are seeking water and there is none; their tongue
> is parched with thirst. I YHWH answer them; I the God of Israel do not
> forsake them.
> I open rivers on the bare hills; fountains in the middle of valleys.
> I turn the wilderness into ponds and the dry land into springs of water
> (41.17-18).[6]

YHWH's explicit assurance of a prosperous future for an attentive Israel strongly implies the devastation, found in the images of water and obliteration, that awaits a disobedient people.

---

3. The first part of the passage was cited above, p. 76, in the discussion of the contrasting meanings of the image of the measuring line and the plummet in 34.11.

4. I am taking the כִּי as emphatic: 'the raging flood, yes! it passes through'.

5. 'Trampled ground', מִרְמָס, alludes to the condition of the vineyard (5.5) and the land (7.25).

6. See above, pp. 16, 102, for other citations of and comments on this passage.

I am YHWH your God who teaches you [masculine singular] how to
  prosper,
Who leads you on the road you should walk on.
O, if only you had paid attention to my commandments!
Then your prosperity would be like a river and your success like the
  waves of the sea.
Your descendants like the sand and your offspring like its grains.
Their name would never be cut off or obliterated from before me (48.17-
  19).

The Close of the Vision: 66.12-24

This latent reading haunts YHWH's final and powerful words of comfort to mother Jerusalem in 66.12-14a and immediately surfaces in vv.
14b-16.

12 For thus says YHWH: 'I am now extending to her peace like a river and,
      like a flooding[7] stream, the wealth of nations,
    And you [masculine plural] will suck and be carried on her hip and
      dandled on her knees.
13 As a man whose mother comforts him,[8] thus I, I comfort you;
      you will find comfort in Jerusalem.
14a You will see and your heart rejoice; your bones will flourish like the grass.'
b   And it will be known that the hand of YHWH is with his servants
      and he is enraged[9] with his enemies.
15 Look! YHWH comes in fire, and like a whirlwind, his chariots,
      To return his anger as fury and his rebuke as flames of fire.
16 Yes, by fire—by his sword—YHWH enters into judgment with all flesh;
      and many are those slain by YHWH.[10]

7. This is the root, שׁטף, that occurs in 28.17-18; I translate it with 'flood' and
'raging'.
8. I translate the phrase literally to stress the presence of the male image in the
midst of the female image of mothering. The first word is אישׁ, not נער, 'child', or
יונק, 'sucking infant' (see 11.6-8). Despite Isaiah's comparatively frequent use of
female imagery, even in association with YHWH, the vision is still male-centered.
The 'you' addressed in this passage are masculine plural, i.e. Jerusalem's sons.
9. In place of MT's qal perfect זעם, BHS suggests a noun with third person
masculine singular suffix, זעמו. This probably reflects a desire to have two nominal
forms in parallel, 'YHWH's hand' and 'his rage'; I keep the MT since it reflects
Isaiah's diversity in his use of parallelism. Most commentaries and translations
accept the BHS proposal either explicitly, e.g. McKenzie and Westermann, or
implicitly, e.g. NAB, NRSV and NJB. JPS follows MT: 'But He shall rage against his
enemies'.
10. See above, p. 16, for other comments on the end of this passage, vv. 15-16.

I conclude my study of Isaiah 34–35 with a reading of the conclusion of the vision of Isaiah in 66.12-24. The conclusion shares much in terminology, themes, imagery and style with our poem and has been frequently cited for parallels. Comfort and anger are juxtaposed, but, unlike our poem that places them in two separate parts, here scenes of peace and prosperity rapidly alternate with those of wrath and death. Pronouns occur and at times with indefinite antecedents. As in our poem, there is no conclusive determination of who, both within and without the vision of Isaiah, the servants and the enemies of YHWH are. Finally, most commentators are troubled by the harshness of the judgments expressed in vv. 15-17 and 24 and by the sharp contrast with the positive tones of the other verses.[11] They propose different interpretations that can involve, first, varying identifications of the pronouns's antecedents and of YHWH's servants and enemies and, secondly, redactional solutions that, depending on the content, ascribe different verses to different authors and stages of the composition of the book.[12]

Verses 12-13, with their explicit concern for YHWH's active comforting of Jerusalem, have little specific relation to our poem, except for the identification of 'you', a masculine plural group. They are Zion's children in v. 8 and, therefore, the Israelites, both in the city and in exile, are the first and most obvious antecedent, but Israel is not mentioned by name in this chapter until the simile in v. 20: 'just as the Israelites bring the gift'. And, in v. 10, 'you' are the more general 'all who love her' and 'all who mourn over her'. 'We' mourn Jerusalem in 63.7–64.11, specifically in 63.18 and 64.9-10; I previously discussed the open and ambiguous identification of 'we' in Isaiah, including parts of ch. 63

---

11. Hanson's comment is representative: 'Odd, though, is the final verse. Concluding the magisterial Book of Isaiah with its celebration of the Holy God whose infinite love reaches out for lost mortals is a verse that holds up as an eternal memorial the worm-infested, smoldering bodies of those who have rebelled against their creator. Modern readers are not the first to flinch at the sight. According to the Masoretic notation, verse 24 is to be followed by the repetition of verse 23 in the synagogue' (1995: 252). Repeating v. 23, however, can have the effect of emphasizing v. 24 by framing it in a chiastic structure.

12. Westermann (1969: 423-29) divides vv. 18-24 into two independent sections, vv. 18-19 and 21 and vv. 20 and 22-24, that contrast a universalist view that goes out to the rest of the world with a particularist view that focuses solely on Zion. Verses 20, 22-24 are 'a deliberate correction of the unprecedent statement made in the former' (Westermann 1969: 423).

(see above, pp. 94-99). Throughout the close of Isaiah's vision, we encounter the double or layered reading in which the focused story of privileged and chosen Israel competes and co-exists with the inclusive story of all humanity. 'You' is as open and plural a category as 'we'.[13]

Verse 14 repeats, in reverse order from 35.1-2, the actions of seeing, רְאֹה, and rejoicing, שִׂישׂ. The heart is rejoicing and no longer trembling as in 35.4; the bones, not the wilderness of 35.1-2, are blooming. YHWH's wrath and hand, in reverse order from 66.14b, frame the first part of our poem in 34.1-17 and, as noted at several points in the reading, the entire poem in chs. 34–35 does not name or distinguish YHWH's servants from his enemies. The recipients of wrath and of joy are not obviously two separate groups or entities. Finally, YHWH is a central, active character at the close of the vision, a role denied him in our poem. In 66.15-16, YHWH, named three times, comes, judges and slays.

Isaiah's penchant for lexical diversity is in evidence in the terms for anger in 66.14-15: זָעַם (he is enraged), אַפּוֹ (his anger), חֵמָה (fury) and גַּעֲרָתוֹ (his rebuke). Of these, only חֵמָה occurs in our poem in 34.2 in parallel with קֶצֶף (see above, p. 30 n. 2), and the only other cluster of four or more terms for anger occurs in the declaration of YHWH's war on the entire world (13.3, 5, 9 and 13). Besides these five terms Isaiah also uses אַכְזָרִי (13.9), זַעַף (30.30), חָרוֹן (13.9, 13) and עברה (e.g. 10.6; 13.9, 13).[14]

Fire, אֵשׁ, occurs three times in 66.15-16. The imagery occurs in 34.9-10a in 'burning pitch', 'not extinguishing' and 'rising smoke'. YHWH's sated and descending sword is a central image in the opening scenes of slaughter in ch. 34 and occurs in close proximity with justice, מִשְׁפָּט; in 66.16 YHWH judges all flesh, נִשְׁפָּט,[15] through his sword. Our poem

---

13. I note the added complexity of gender and number with the second person. In Isaiah 'you' can be masculine or feminine and singular or plural; the feminine plural, for example, occurs in 32.9-12. YHWH doesn't address just his servants as 'you', but also his enemies: 'You who abandon YHWH, who forget my holy mountain...I destine you to the sword and all of you bow to the slaughter' (65.11-12). Note the parallels in this passage with 34.2-7: slaughter (טבח), sword and 'going down'—'bowing' (34.7).

14. For discussion of עברה, including the root play on its consonants, see above, p. 73 n. 57.

15. The niphal perfect, נִשְׁפָּט, produces a rhyme with the noun מִשְׁפָּט; I reiterate that Isaiah's choice of specific forms can be for poetic as much as for grammatical and syntactical reasons (see above, p. 39).

opens with the sight, in 34.3, of the slain, חללים, and their corpses, פגרים (see 66.24).

> Those who are sanctifying and cleansing themselves to go into gardens,
> following one in the center,[16] are eating the flesh of swine, vermin and
> mice; they come to an end together—saying of YHWH (66.17).

The passage is similar to 65.3-7 in its depiction of illicit rites conducted in gardens and involving unclean animals and in its parody of
being holy and clean. 'Those who say [to YHWH], "Keep to yourself;
don't come near me for I'm too holy for you"' (65.5).[17] I discussed the
priestly overtones of both holy or sanctified, קדש, and clean or pure,
טהר, in connection with the close of our poem where the unclean, טמא,
the opposite of the clean, do not wander onto the Holy Way (see above,
pp. 109-110). Finally, I commented on the passage as part of Isaiah's
encyclopedic treatment of animals (see above, pp. 55-56 n. 34); despite
using almost 100 different terms for animals throughout the book,
'vermin', שקץ, and 'mice', עקבר, are *hapax legomena*.

But who are these people who are sanctifying themselves? Are they
YHWH's enemies who are contrasted with his servants in 66.14 and
65.9-15? Or are they part of the general 'all flesh' in 66.16 whom
YHWH judges and of whom he slays many? Even here at the close of
the book, where we might expect a definitive resolution, we encounter
the ambiguity of deciding exactly who YHWH is for and against and we
encounter manifest and latent readings.

> I, their deeds and their thoughts, it/she is coming to gather all the nations
> and the tongues; they come and see my glory (66.18).

As with my treatment of 34.16c (see above, p. 86 n. 92), I discuss
possibilities for reading the opening phrase in 66.18 but do not offer an

16. The Ketib is אחד, 'one' masculine, while the Qere and 1QIsaᵃ have אחת,
'one' feminine. This is probably a reference to a priest (or priestess if we accept the
Qere) or other cultic leader. Ezek. 8.7-13 describes a scene of abominable cultic
worship in the temple, conducted by 70 elders with 'Jaazaniah son of Shaphan
standing in their midst' (v. 11).

17. The final word, קְדַשְׁתִּיךְ, a qal perfect with suffix, is a difficult form and
'I'm too holy for you' is an approximation. Watts renders 'I am set apart from you'
(1987: 339). *BHS* suggests reading piel perfect, קִדַּשְׁתִּיךְ, that JPS adopts 'For I
would render you consecrated' and notes the other reading. Watts (1987: 341)
tellingly comments on the qal and piel forms: 'Both meanings are ambiguous'. I
think that part of the difficulty derives from the fact that the verb is being used in a
satirical sense.

emended text that I would not then defend. Muilenburg, who notes 'The opening of the verse is corrupt, and many conjectures have been proposed' (1956: 770), takes a similar approach; he discusses some of the conjectures but proposes no textual solution of his own. Watts (1987: 361, 364) discusses both the evidence of the versions and the proposed emendations.

The LXX and Syriac add יַדַעְתִּי after 'I'; this reading is adopted by JPS, KJV, NRSV and REB. JPS and REB, following a change first proposed by Duhm, place the phrase 'for I know their deeds and their thoughts' at the end of v. 17 with a break between it and v. 18b while NRSV keeps it as the opening of v. 18: 'For I know their works and their thoughts, and I am coming to gather all nations'.[18] Watts adds an interpretive, parenthetical term: 'And I (*despite*) their deeds and their thoughts, coming to gather all the nations' (1987: 359). NIV renders it analogously but with the opposite sense of 'despite': 'And I, because of their actions and their imaginations, am about to come'. (In both quotations the emphasis is mine.)

A second problem with the opening of v. 18 is that the antecedent of 'their' is not specified and is, as with many of the pronouns in our poem, ambiguous. Many connect it with the sinners in v. 17, for example, Westermann (1969: 422) who moves the phrase there: 'those who sanctify and purify themselves to go into the garden... [their thoughts and their deeds] shall come to an end together'.[19] However, since the identity of these sinners in v. 17 is ambiguous, this identification does not resolve the problem at the start of v. 18. Others connect 'their' with the following nations and tongues whether it is because of (NIV) or despite (Watts) their thoughts that YHWH is advancing.

NIV makes the connection evident. 'And I, because of their actions and their imaginations, am about to come and gather all nations and tongues'. However, in the NIV Study Edition (1985: 1114), the editors add a footnote that interprets the passage in a quite different sense. 'Wicked Israelites may be the antecedent'. This confusion, Israelites or nations, is reflective of the multiple meanings of the close of the vision

18. *BHS* suggests moving the phrase to v. 16c after 'all flesh' as additional objects of YHWH's judgment. In these suggestions the translators are apparently taking כִּי, 'for', from the final letters of אָנֹכִי, 'I'.

19. JPS, Conrad (1991: 92-95) and McKenzie (1968: 206) have a similar reading.

of Isaiah and not of just the initial words of v. 18. The close shares much with our poem in terms of polysemy and openness.

The fourth term in the verse is also problematic. בָּאָה is a feminine singular participle with no obvious subject; I reflect the ambiguity in my rendering 'it/she'. In the context 'I', at the start of the verse, is certainly YHWH. LXX and other ancient versions read a masculine singular participle בָּא to fit with 'I', YHWH; this is adopted by most translators. JPS, however, keeps the MT and supplies a feminine subject 'time', עת, and marks the conjecture with brackets: '[The time] has come to gather all the nations'. KJV has a related rendering: 'it shall come, that I will gather all nations'.

However, I think that, even given these textual problems and ambiguities, we can say that the opening of v. 18 is spoken by YHWH, as is the rest of the close of the vision, about 'them' and their deeds and about the nations. 'They', the antecedent of 'their', may be Israelites, the nations or all flesh—and any of these may be considered wicked or righteous—as a category subsuming these two groups. Even in the confines of v. 18 it is not demanded by the text that 'they' and the nations be synonymous. YHWH or some manifestation of him, for example, his spirit/breath as in 34.16 or his anger, עברה (to have a feminine noun in agreement with בָּאָה), is coming to gather all the nations and tongues.[20]

In a more focused action YHWH 'will collect the outcasts of Israel; the dispersed of Judah he will gather from the four corners of the earth' (11.12). In a contrasting use of 'to gather', the poet describes the day of YHWH's wrath as a time when all scatter 'like sheep with no one to gather them' (13.14). In our poem, vultures gathered in the demonic land and YHWH's breath or spirit gathered others (34.15-16; see above, pp. 86 and 88). The term is comparatively frequent in chs. 40–66. Unlike the time of wrath, YHWH is coming to Judah to gather his flock in his arms (40.11; see 43.5). All the nations gather to hear YHWH present his case against other gods and their idols (43.9; 45.20; 48.14). The children of the desolate woman, Zion or another, are gathered to her (49.18; 54.7; 60.4).

In 56.1-8 the prophet proclaims that any, represented by the foreigner and eunuch, who keep the covenant may join themselves to YHWH.

---

20. 'Nations and tongues' occurs, as a phrase, in Zech. 8.23 and in Aramaic in Dan. 3.4, 7, 29 and 6.26. In Joel 4.2 (3.2 Eng.) YHWH announces 'I will gather all the nations'.

All who keep the sabbath by not profaning it and hold fast to my
    covenant:
I bring them to my holy mountain and make them happy in my house of
    prayer;
Their burnt offerings and their sacrifices are acceptable on my altar;
My house is certainly called A House of Prayer for All The Peoples—
A saying of Adonai YHWH, who gathers the outcasts of Israel—
'I am still gathering more to it besides its/his gathered' (56.7-8).[21]

I cite the passage at length because of its other ties to the close of
Isaiah's vision and will return to it as we progress in our reading.[22]
YHWH's place is his holy mountain, his altar and his house of prayer, a
house that is for all the peoples.

The use of a participle, 'who gathers', emphasizes that this is a con-
tinuous activity on YHWH's part and not a once-and-for-all action (see
Westermann 1969: 315). 'The outcasts of Israel' parallel 'the dispersed
of Judah' in 11.12 cited immediately above. 'I am still gathering more'
renders the imperfective force of the *yiqtol* verb that describes 'a *process* (rather than an event)' and that focuses on the 'internal distinctions
of various separate phases making up the situation' (Waltke and
O'Connor 1990: 480; see above, p. 32). The imperfectivity matches the
continuity of the participle: YHWH is always gathering the outcasts of
Israel and of all humanity.

To return to the close of the vision, those gathered 'come and see my
glory' (66.18). This is reminiscent of the transformation described in
35.1-2:

21. The final line offers at least one, if not two, examples of a pronoun with an
open antecedent. I render the first one, a third person masculine singular suffix on a
preposition, עָלָיו, with 'it', a reference to YHWH's place, his house of prayer;
others, e.g. Watts, Westermann, NAB, NRSV and REB, take it as a reference to Israel.
'Others will I gather to him besides those already gathered' (NAB). The second
pronoun, a third person masculine singular suffix on the niphal participle, נִקְבָּצָיו,
can be 'its gathered ones' referring to YHWH's place or 'his gathered ones'
referring either to YHWH himself or to Israel. I mark the ambiguity with the virgule:
'its/his'. We again have a plural text with several readings, e.g. only Israel or all the
nations, enclosed within it.

22. Hanson comments: 'Isaiah 56.1-8 is one half of a literary framework that
encloses Third Isaiah, the other half being found in 66.18-23...as in 56.7 God
announced, "My house shall be called a house of prayer for all peoples", in 66.23
God says, "All flesh shall come to worship before me"' (1995: 196). Both are
marked by cultic imagery.

The glory of the Lebanon is given to her,
  the splendor of the Carmel and the Sharon.
They see the glory of YHWH,
  the splendor of our God.

And, matching the openness and plurality of our poem, YHWH continues his proclamation at the close of Isaiah employing both nouns and pronouns that have multiple references.

I place a sign among them and I send survivors [פלטים] from them to the nations—Tarshish, Pul[23] and Lud (those who draw the bow),[24] Tubal and Javan—the far coastlands that have not heard of my fame [שמעי] or seen my glory. And they will proclaim my glory to the nations (66.19).

A sign, אות, has parallels in Isaiah, for example, in the sign given to Ahaz (7.11-14), Isaiah's walking naked (20.3), the signs given to Hezekiah (37.30 and 38.7, 22) and the open-ended proclamation that closes ch. 55. The latter begins with והיה that 'introduces a discussion or…advances it by introducing a situation that is only more or less loosely connected with the preceding situation (Waltke and O'Connor 1990: 538-39; see above, p. 61).

And it serves for YHWH as a memorial and as an everlasting sign [אות עולם] that will not be cut off (55.13).

Watts (1987: 365) comments on 66.19 that 'Here the sign is not defined'; he maintains that it can be both Israelite survivors in Jerusalem and a remnant among the nations. Conrad (1991: 93) argues for the former and notes that the sign offered to Hezekiah relates to the escape of a band of survivors, פליטה, from Mount Zion (37.30-32; see 4.2). Westermann (1969: 425) defends the latter and points to the gathering (קבץ) of 'the survivors of the nations', פליטי הגוים, in 45.20.

The ambiguity, the double reading, derives chiefly from the third

---

23. LXX and many translations read פוט, 'Put', as in Jer. 46.9.

24. For MT משכי, 'drawers-of', LXX reads 'Mosoch' for which *BHS* suggests reading מֶשֶׁךְ, 'Meshech'. Some, e.g. McKenzie, Westermann, NJB and REB, accept the latter; NAB renders 'Mosoch'. LXX omits MT קשת, 'bow'; those who accept the deletion, e.g. NAB and NJB, would argue that the term 'bow' was added because of the parallel to drawing the bow in Jer. 46.9. Duhm (cited in Westermann 1969: 426) originally suggested reading ראש, 'Rosh', in place of קשת since Rosh is listed with Meshek and Tubal in Ezek. 38.2 and 39.1. The emendation is accepted by some, e.g. McKenzie, Westermann and REB. NIV creatively renders the whole phrase 'drawers of the bow' as 'famous as archers'.

masculine plural pronouns in the prepositional phrases 'among *them*', בהם, and 'from *them*', מהם. 'They' can be Israelites, the nations or all humanity without national distinction. Westermann (1969: 425) maintains that the antecedent of 'them' in the phrases is the same and that YHWH sends a remnant from one part of the nations to another, even more distant, part of the nations. Conrad (1991: 94) rejects this and asserts that YHWH sends survivors from Israel or Jerusalem to the nations. This division of opinion is similar to the debate surrounding 49.1-6 where apparently servant Israel is sent to restore Israel. The text supports both readings at the same time and, at the close of Isaiah's vision, we again encounter the double or layered reading in which the focused story of privileged and chosen Israel, Westermann's particularist view, competes and co-exists with the inclusive story of all humanity, his universalist view (see above, p. 126 n. 12). The inclusiveness is underlined by the list of actual nations.

Not only do these distant lands finally hear of YHWH and see his glory but they then tell of it (הגידו) to or among the nations. This is analogous to the proclamation (√נגד) of YHWH's wondrous deeds announced in the psalms (e.g. 9.12; 22.32; 71.17-18 and 145.4). It is also similar to the situation in the second part of our poem where, after the assertion that 'they' see YHWH's glory, we read the actual proclamation of YHWH's approach and its effects: strength, fearlessness and vengeance (35.2-4). In the relation of the general and the particular, the rest of humanity, individually or as a group, acts just as Israel and Israelites do or, from the reverse perspective, Israel acts as the rest of humanity does.

In 35.2-4 the poet spoke of 'we', 'you' (masculine plural) and 'they'; here he presents 'I' (YHWH), 'they' (one or more groups) and 'you' (masculine plural). In both places we can describe the relationships that exist between the entities referred to with the pronouns without having to identify each one with another named entity in Isaiah.

> *They* bring all *your* kin from all the nations as a gift to YHWH—on horses, in chariots, in wagons, on asses and on camels[25]—on *my* holy

25. This list is similar to the list of nations in the preceding verse, and it vividly presents the scene of the returning bands. Both lists permit Isaiah to demonstrate his encyclopedic grasp of the world and of the Hebrew language.

> mountain Jerusalem, says YHWH, just as the Israelites[26] bring the gift,[27]
> in clean vessels, to YHWH's house. And *I* even take *from them* some to
> be priests and Levites, says YHWH (66.20-21).

'They' is open to the same different readings—Israelites, the nations
or all humanity without national distinction—as in v. 19. Muilenburg
(1956: 772) comments on the ambiguity of 'from them': 'Whether of
the Diaspora or of the nations is not clear'. As in 66.12-14 masculine
plural 'you' of 'your kin' refers first to the Israelites, but there is the
lingering possibility that 'you' are the nations whom indefinite 'they'
are bringing to YHWH as a gift, perhaps as tribute. This reading is supported by the use of the third person by YHWH or the poet at the close
of v. 20—'says YHWH, just as the Israelites bring the gift, in clean ves-
sels, to YHWH's house'—in a comment that contrasts the Israelites with
'you'.

The passage shares cultic imagery with 56.7-8[28] in which YHWH
speaks of his holy mountain as his house of prayer and of burnt offerings and sacrifices[29] on his altar. I discussed the cultic and priestly
categories of 'clean' and 'unclean' in relation to the holy way at the
close of our poem (see above, pp. 109-110). The holy way leads to
Zion, a site of joy and song; in ch. 66 YHWH refers to 'my holy mountain Jerusalem' that, to some extent, stands separate from 'YHWH's
house' in the subsequent comment. 'My holy mountain Jerusalem' is,
at the same time, the city of Jerusalem, YHWH's abode, and the ideal
place and state that YHWH's servants, both Israelites and foreigners,
seek to come to and to dwell in. Further analyses of Isaiah need to pay
close attention to the descriptions and roles of Jerusalem, Zion and
YHWH's house addressing issues such as: Where are they equated and
where are they distinguished from one another? Who are they associated with: YHWH, Israel or the nations? Where are they spoken of as

26. The phrase בני ישראל, sons of Israel, is not frequent in Isaiah and occurs
elsewhere only in 17.3 and 9, 27.12 and 31.6.

27. 'Gift', מנחה, connotes a present or tribute in its first occurrence; see Gen.
32.14, 1 Kgs 5.1, 2 Kgs 8.8 and 17.3-4 for this usage. In its second occurrence, it
connotes an offering or sacrifice; see Gen. 4.3-5, Exod. 29.41 and 1 Kgs 8.64 for
this usage.

28. See above, p. 131, for citation and discussion of the passage and p. 131
n. 22 for Hanson's comments on the parallels between 56.1-8 and 66.18-23.

29. The Hebrew words are עולות and זבחים. 'Sacrifices on my altar [מזבח]'
takes on a chilling note through the shadow text of the 'sacrifice [זבח] for YHWH'
announced in 34.6 amid imagery of sword, blood and slaughter (טבח).

historical sites and as ideal sites or states?

YHWH's declaration that he will even take *some of them* (מֵהֶם) as priests and Levites continues both the cultic motif and the double reading since 'them' is Israelite and/or foreigner. This is reminiscent of the nations streaming 'to the mountain of YHWH's house' (2.2) and of the foreigners (בני הנכר) whose 'burnt offerings and sacrifices are acceptable on my altar' (56.7).

The vision of Isaiah closes with memorable scenes of universal worship and of smoldering corpses. The passage is similar to our poem in its juxtaposition of the grand and the grim.

> As the new heavens and the new earth, which I am making,
> stand before me—saying of YHWH—so does your seed and your name stand.
> And further from new moon to new moon and from sabbath to sabbath,[30]
> All flesh comes to bow down before me, says YHWH,
> And they go out and see the bodies of the people who rebel against me,
> For their worm never dies; their fire is never to be quenched; and finally, they are a horror to all flesh (66.22-24).

As above, masculine plural 'you' of 'your seed and name' refers first to the Israelites, but with the possibility that 'you' are the nations who bring the gift to YHWH and then stand before him in perpetual worship. 'And further' attempts to capture the impact of the initial והיה that introduces a new situation only loosely related to what precedes (see above, pp. 61 and 132). The worship by 'all flesh' is an advance on the persistence of 'your seed and your name' and not a simple parallel. 'All flesh' is the inclusive category, first introduced in 40.5-6, for all people, and perhaps even including animals at some points. It is used three times at the close of the book and the usage attests to the range of Isaiah's vision. All flesh is judged by YHWH (v. 16); all flesh bows before YHWH (v. 23); all flesh is disgusted at the rebels's corpses (v. 24).

'And they go out and see' reflects the use of two *weqatals*—ויצאו וראו—in sequence with the preceding *yiqtol*—יבוא—and the imperfectivity, the focus on the process and stages of the actions, of the

---

30. The second 'new moon' and 'sabbath' both have the third person masculine singular pronominal suffix: 'its new moon' and 'its sabbath'. Watts (1987: 360-61) translates literally: 'And it will be from a new moon to its (following) new moon, and from a sabbath to its (following) sabbath'.

latter carries over to the former. We are presented a vivid scene as we watch all flesh repeatedly coming to worship YHWH and then going out to view the dead bodies of those 'who rebel against me'. The participle 'rebels', הפשעים, connotes the ongoing nature of rebellion; these aren't just people who rebelled in the past. Apparently the new heavens and the new earth do not mean that all the evils of the past are gone. 'And finally', similar to the preceding 'and further', renders the initial והיה that stresses the final phrase by making it other than just one in a series.

The closing scene is analogous to seeing the Holy Way in 35.8-10 surrounded by the demonic realm and creatures of 34.8-14 (see above, pp. 111-12). It is similar to reading the poem in Isaiah 34–35 as a single vision that juxtaposes, as contemporary, the demonic realm of wrath and the transformed wilderness of joy. Here, however, the dream and the nightmare are presented in the opposite order of our poem. The poem ended with the flight of grief and moaning, and Isaiah's whole vision ends with a scene of perdition: undying worms, perpetual fire and finally 'a horror for all flesh'.

BIBLIOGRAPHY

Aichele, G., and T. Pippin (eds.)
1992   'Fantasy and the Bible', *Semeia* 60.
1997   'Special Issue: Fantasy and the Bible', *JFA* 8.2.
Aichele, G.
1997   'Fantasy and the Gospels: Theological and Ideological Implications',
            JFA 8: 170-84.
Barthes, R.
1974   *S/Z* (trans. R. Miller; New York: Hill and Wang).
Barton, J.
1995   *Isaiah 1–39* (OTG; Sheffield: Sheffield Academic Press).
Clines, D.J.A.
1976   *I, He, We, and They: A Literary Approach to Isaiah 53* (JSOTSup, 1;
            Sheffield: JSOT Press).
Conrad, E.W.
1991   *Reading Isaiah* (Minneapolis: Fortress Press).
Freud, S.
1965   *The Interpretation of Dreams* (trans. J. Strachey; New York: Avon Books
            [1900]).
1976   'The "Uncanny"' (trans. J. Strachey), *New Literary History* 7: 619-45.
Frye, N.
1957   *Anatomy of Criticism* (Princeton, NJ: Princeton University Press).
Hanson, P.D.
1995   *Isaiah 40–66* (Interpretation; Louisville, KY: Westminster/John Knox
            Press).
Kaiser, O.
1974   *Isaiah 13–39* (trans. R. Wilson; OTL; Philadelphia: Westminster Press).
Lack, R.
1973   *La symbolique du livre d'Isaïe* (AnBib, 59; Rome: Biblical Institute
            Press).
Lust, Johan
1989   'Isaiah 34 and the *herem*', in J. Vermeylen (ed.), *Le livre d'Isaïe: Les
            oracles et leurs relectures: Unité et complexité de l'ouvrage* (BETL, 81;
            Leuven: Leuven University Press): 275-86.
Mathews, C.R.
1995   *Defending Zion: Edom's Desolation and Jacob's Restoration (Isaiah 34–
            35) in Context* (New York: W. de Gruyter).
McKenzie, J.L.
1968   *Second Isaiah* (AB, 20; Garden City, NY: Doubleday, 1968).

Miscall, P.D.
1991   'Isaiah: The Labyrinth of Images', *Semeia* 54: 103-21.
1992a   'Biblical Narrative and Categories of the Fantastic', *Semeia* 60: 39-51.
1992b   'Isaiah: New Heavens, New Earth, New Book', in D.N. Fewell (ed.),
              Reading between Texts (Louisville, KY: Westminster/John Knox Press):
              41-56.
1993   *Isaiah* (Readings; Sheffield: JSOT Press).
1995   'Texts, More Texts, a Textual Reader, and a Textual Writer', *Semeia*
              69/70: 247-60.
1997   'Isaiah: Dreams and Nightmares, Fantasy and Horror', *JFA* 8: 151-69.
Muilenburg, J.
1940   'The Literary Character of Isaiah 34', *JBL* 59: 339-65.
1984   'The Literary Character of Isaiah 34', reprinted in T.F. Best (ed.),
              *Hearing and Speaking the Word: Selections from the Works of James
              Muilenberg* (Homage Series; Chico, CA: Scholars Press): 59-85.
1956   'The Book of Isaiah, Chapters 40-66', in *The Interpreters Bible*, V
              (Nashville: Abingdon Press): 381-773.
Niccacci, A.
1997   'Analysing Biblical Hebrew Poetry', *JSOT* 74: 77-93.
Petersen, D.L., and K.H. Richards
1992   *Interpreting Hebrew Poetry* (Guides to Biblical Scholarship;
              Minneapolis: Augsburg–Fortress).
Pippin, T.
1997   'Apocalyptic Horror', *JFA* 8: 198-217.
Roberts, J.J.M.
1987   'Yahweh's Foundations in Zion (Isa. 28.16)', *JBL* 106: 27-45.
Sawyer, J.F.A.
1989   'Daughter of Zion and Servant of the Lord in Isaiah: A Comparison',
              JSOT 44: 89-108.
1995   'The Ethics of Comparative Interpretation', *Currents in Research:
              Biblical Studies* 3: 153-68.
Scott, R.B.Y.
1956   'The Book of Isaiah, Chapters 1–39', in *The Interpreters Bible*, V
              (Nashville: Abingdon Press): 149-381.
Seitz, C.R.
1993   *Isaiah 1–39* (Interpretation; Louisville, KY: Westminster/John Knox
              Press).
Todorov, T.
1973   *The Fantastic: A Structural Approach to a Literary Genre* (trans. R.
              Howard; Cleveland: Case Western Reserve University Press).
Tromp, N.J.
1969   *Primitive Conceptions of Death and the Nether World in the Old
              Testament* (*BO*, 21; Rome: Biblical Institute Press).
Twitchell, J.B.
1985   *Dreadful Pleasures: An Anatomy of Modern Horror* (New York: Oxford
              University Press).

Waltke, B.K., and M. O'Connor
1990   *An Introduction to Biblical Hebrew Syntax* (Winona Lake, IN: Eisenbrauns).

Watson, G.E.W.
1984   *Classical Hebrew Poetry: A Guide to its Techniques* (JSOTSup, 26; Sheffield: JSOT Press).

Watts, J.D.W.
1985   *Isaiah 1–33* (WBC, 24; Waco, TX: Word Books).
1987   *Isaiah 34–66* (WBC, 25; Waco, TX: Word Books).

Webb, B.G.
1990   'Zion in Transformation: A Literary Approach to Isaiah', in D.J.A. Clines, S.E. Fowl and S.E. Porter (eds.), *The Bible in Three Dimensions* (JSOTSup, 87; Sheffield: JSOT Press): 93-108.

Westermann, C.
1969   *Isaiah 40–66* (trans. D.M.G. Stalker; OTL; Philadelphia: Westminster Press).

White, Hayden
1973   *Metahistory: The Historical Imagination in Nineteenth-Century Europe* (Baltimore: The Johns Hopkins University Press).
1978   *The Tropics of Discourse: Essays in Cultural Criticism* (Baltimore: The Johns Hopkins University Press).

Wildberger, H.
1972   *Jesaja 1–12* (BKAT, 10.1; Neukirchen–Vluyn: Neukirchener Verlag).
1982   *Jesaja 28–39* (BKAT 10.3; Neukirchen–Vluyn: Neukirchener Verlag).

INDEXES

INDEX OF REFERENCES

INDEX OF AUTHORS

JOURNAL FOR THE STUDY OF THE OLD TESTAMENT
SUPPLEMENT SERIES